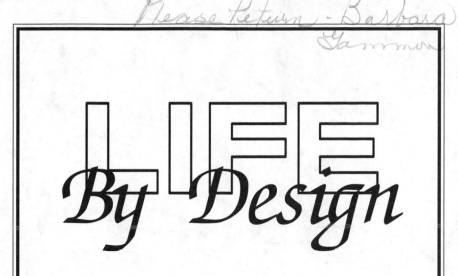

BOOK 3

A Guide to Personal Devotions and Daily Bible Study

by
Dr. Don Hill

Special 100 Huntley Street Edition
Published by Lay Leadership International

July 19/98

Read = In every situation God is is our life moment to moment
2 Corinthians 4 - 16 - 18

1960's Re = Gary Coleman Story - Day of Discovery (United States airforce)
For the Disheartened. Downtrodden
Incredible life story - uplifting

The statistics used in "Today's World Prayer Emphasis," as well as some of the prayer requests, were adapted from Patrick Johnstone's *Operation World: The Day-by-Day Guide to Praying for the World*. Zondervan Publishing House, Grand Rapids: 1993.

ISBN: 0-88151-238-9

SPECIAL EDITION OF LIFE BY DESIGN - BOOK 3
By Don E. Hill
Published by Lay Leadership International
Danville, Kentucky

100 HUNTLEY
STREET

Dear Fellow *Life by Design* Participant:

This is number three of eight volumes. As president of Crossroads Communication and producer for *Life by Design*, I search diligently and prayerfully for Bible study materials which will help all who look to us for ministry. I have "others" in mind. But this series is helpful for me, too, in a very special way.

As I write these words, this Ministry is in a "fiery furnace." The Lord is purifying and strengthening us. He's there with us as the fourth man was there for and with the Three Hebrew Children. I know that because of His presence, we will come forth as gold, not having bowed to the idols of worldly maneuvering and manipulation, but strong in the miracles and marvels of our great God and Savior, Jesus Christ.

Therefore, I know with complete assurance, that once again in this new volume, God will use the excellent teaching gifts of Don Hill to continue to minister powerfully to us all.

In Christ's love and service,

David Mainse
President
Crossroads Christian Communications, Inc.

A NOTE FROM THE AUTHOR

Blessed are the meek for they will inherit the earth.

What a strange paradox! To many, meekness is associated with weakness. Yet for the Christian, meekness is the strength that will ultimately win the world for Jesus Christ—the One who said, "I am meek" (Mt. 11:29). Now in the third Beatitude, He extends a call to disciples of all generations to emulate this characteristic for His sake.

Throughout His life and ministry, Christ showed the key to meekness—complete submission to the will of God and His authority. As we will see, being broken to the reign and rule of God is an essential part of the spiritual development of the person who claims to be a man or woman of God.

Christ also showed meekness through humility. He left the highest position of all to be born in a lowly stable into a peasant home, and to die the most socially disreputable of all deaths. Why? So He could redeem and serve a lost, bruised, and hurting world. Likewise, He asks us to humble ourselves and be a servant of all those who are in need.

Finally, Christ showed meekness by being gentle even to His enemies. In Gethsemane, Peter retaliated against Christ's enemies by cutting off the ear of a Roman soldier. Christ restored the ear and admonished Peter. Forceful retaliation is not the way of the Cross. We win people to Christ only by loving those who, more often than not, tend to reject us.

Obviously meekness entails much more than we can ever hope to achieve on our own. Meekness is a fruit of the Spirit. It's one of those qualities that the Holy Spirit is seeking to produce in us. We are often like Peter. Our old nature tends to want to conquer by force, manipulation, coercion, and deception. Only with the help of the Holy Spirit can we overcome these temptations and follow God's way of love, humility, and gentleness.

A paradox? Yes, but when all the world's great conquering leaders have come and gone, only the meek will truly inherit the earth.

Blessed are they that hunger and thirst for righteousness,
for they shall be filled.

In this volume we will also address this fourth Beatitude. Although only a few lessons are devoted to it, this concept is by no means less important than any other. In fact, spiritual hunger is the primary factor that determines our growth in Christ. Unless it is cultivated, our desire to be like Christ will stagnate and eventually die.

The people who first heard these words knew exactly what Jesus meant. They lived by the desert and many had experienced all too often the intense pangs of starvation and dehydration. Jesus chose words from His own language that meant a type of spiritual hunger and thirst that was indeed intense.

However, such a passionate desire for righteousness is not automatic. In the closing lessons of this volume, we will discover from the Word of God what is necessary to maintain an insatiable hunger for God.

May God give you an increased hunger to know Jesus Christ more fully as you continue along the path of growing in His character so aptly described in these Beatitudes.

— Don Hill

ACKNOWLEDGEMENTS

A special thanks to some special associates who continue to be so instrumental in the creation of the *Life by Design* series: to my wife, Carol for her devotion to seeing the project accomplished and her many hours of proofreading; to Sue Montgomery, a gifted editor and writer who takes my rough drafts and organizes them into words that communicate so effectively; to David Mainse, president of Crossroads Christian Communications, who continues to give the series the kind of visibility and credence it needs to touch so many lives for Christ; and finally, to Val Dodd, LLI director, and others on both the LLI and Crossroads staff who are laboring so faithfully to make the series a success.

GETTING THE MOST OUT OF
YOUR DEVOTIONAL GUIDE

Every day, Monday through Friday:

VIEW - The 3-minute devotional segment offered on the *100 Huntley Street* telecast.

READ - The accompanying devotional lesson guide for the day.

STUDY - Answer the Bible study questions and get into God's Word for yourself.

PRAY - Each day we have included a Prayer Emphasis to guide you in praying for a specific country of the world. In addition, there is a weekend prayer guide, plus a special "God is Faithful Prayer List" page in the back of the book on which you add your faith requests and record the answers.

MEET - If at all possible, meet once a week with friends to discuss your completed Bible study questions and Weekend Journal reflections.

Weekends: Turn to your weekend Devotional Guide and Journal.

Further suggestions for use:

- Use the guide as a Sunday school quarterly, studying the Guide five days a week and using the Sunday school hour to discuss the subjects studied during the previous week.

- Use the Guide as a basis for a small group Bible study in your church or home.

All Scripture quotations taken from the New International Version[1] unless otherwise indicated.

---

[1] New International Version Copyright © 1978 by New York International Bible Society.

TABLE OF CONTENTS

Blessed Are the Meek
Blessed Are They that Hunger and Thirst
for Righteousness

Section I:

A study that introduces the concept of meekness and its overall meaning. Since meekness has much to say about God's authorities on earth, individuals are shown how to correctly interpret and yield to God's highest authority— His Word.

Lessons 1 - 20

Section II:

A continuing study showing how God desires His people to relate in a spirit of meekness to His ordained human authorities in government, the home, and the Church. Also included is another important authority—the leading of God's Holy Spirit. Answers to how the believer handles conflicts that arise between these authorities are thoroughly investigated.

Lessons 21 - 40

SectionIII:

The first part is a continuing study on how the meek person relates to people during the daily course of life. Questions about what it means to be humble and gentle are addressed. The second part introduces the fourth Beatitude—Spiritual Hunger. Individuals are shown how this Beatitude provides the necessary motivation for a believer's on-going growth in Christ.

Lessons 41-65

Section I:

Understanding Meekness and God's Highest Authority

"Blessed are the meek,
for they will inherit the earth"
Matthew 5:5

In this third Beatitude, Jesus has shown us how we should relate to His leadership in the world, as well as how we should treat our peers and lead others.

Often, the biblical perspective on love and authority proves difficult because it conflicts with the strong values of individualism we have learned from modern society.

The message of Christ, however, is balanced. He has called us to know how distinctively talented and gifted we are. At the same time, He has shown us how we must relate to the whole of His creation.

The first step toward meekness is to surrender to the one and only authority in this imperfect world that will never fail us—God's Word.

Lesson 1

BLESSED ARE THE MEEK:
The Essential Attitude of Discipleship

"Blessed are the meek, for they will inherit the earth" (Mt. 5:5).

THE DISCIPLE
Body
Soul
Spirit
Christ in You

To this point we have presented two principles relative to effective Christian living and ministry—the essential foundation for all ministry, poverty of spirit and how God trains and molds His servants into the image of Christ through spiritual mourning

Now we enter the third principle of effective Christian living and ministry—meekness, the primary result of spiritual mourning. Meekness deals with your vertical (upward) relationship to God and your horizontal (outward) relationships with other people. In a nutshell, meekness entails gentleness toward both God and man.

Meekness is difficult to comprehend, let alone practice. How can you actually love your enemies, turn the other cheek, and go the second mile? Clearly, it must be a work of God's Holy Spirit in your heart. Our Father has willed that His work must go forward, not by force, but in the gentleness and love of Christ. Most often when God's people have failed to glorify Him, it has been because of their inability to be meek.

The diagram shows that when the Holy Spirit has come into your life, He desires to renew every aspect of your being. The outline of the church signifies how God uses His body of believers to assist this inner work of the Holy Spirit.

When the Holy Spirit comes to live in you, He brings the very character and mind of Jesus Christ (1 Cor. 2:15-16).

The arrows pointing outward from the inner character of Christ show how the Holy Spirit continues to renew your mind and conform it to His own. The heavier arrows pointing inward indicate the Christ-like influence of fellow believers who assist the work of the Holy Spirit in conforming us to the image of Christ.

God desires to make you meek as Jesus is meek. As you cultivate your relationship with God, the meek spirit of Christ within you begins to affect

2

Rom 10-13 Whoever calls on the name of the Lord shall be saved.

your personality. He deals with you about your submission to God's will and authority and with setting aside your own personal rights to serve the higher law of love toward all people.

This is the secret of winning the world to Christ and overcoming every obstacle. The meek will indeed inherit the earth.

■■

BIBLE STUDY GUIDE

Today's Bible Reading:
Matt. 11:29; 1 Cor. 2:16; Gal. 5:22 23

1. What did Christ say about Himself in Matthew 11:29? _I am gentle and humble in Spirit_

2. How do believers know that this same quality of Christ is within them? 1Cor. 2:16 _15 - Whoever has the Spirit is able to judge the value of everything we however have the mind of Christ_

3. As the Holy Spirit renews our minds or thinking, certain new qualities or fruit emerge in our lives. Is the quality of Christ we are studying mentioned as part of the Holy Spirit's fruit? Gal. 5:22-23 _Yes - Spirit produces love joy peace patience kindness goodness faithfulness humility - self control -_

TODAY'S WORLD PRAYER EMPHASIS

AFRICA - ST. HELENA & ASCENSION
- Population: 8,000
- Religion: Non-religious/other 2.8%; Baha'i 0.5%; Christian 96.7%
- Needs:
    Pray for the full evangelization of this generation of islanders. Over the past 30 years there has been a dramatic decline in church attendance. Consequently, St. Helenan society is hedonistic and indifferent to the claims of the gospel.
    Pray for a restoration of strong Christian families which are being adversely affected by the unstable patterns of their society.

Lesson 2

MEEKNESS MEANS SUBMISSION

The first aspect of meekness deals with our submission to God's authority on earth.

The Greek word for meekness, *praus*, means a soft, gentle, and tamed spirit which is openly submissive to God.

Praus was a term used to describe the taming of a wild horse or animal whose strength had to be channeled into something constructive and usable.

In the disciple who is truly meek, the rebellious will has been given over to God and is now submitted to God's authority in heaven and on earth.

Embodied in this attitude is the desire to be totally submitted to God's sovereignty, God's Word, God's human authorities, as well as the inner leading of the Holy Spirit.

I grew up on a small acreage and my father loved horses. He had a reputation in the neighborhood for being able to break just about any spirited young colt. Occasionally, neighbors would bring their young horses to him.

As a young boy I remember my father telling me that the aim was never to break a horse's spirit, only to channel its tremendous energy. Once a horse was broken to the reins of its master, then its power could be put to great use. *Re: Teens*

So it is in our Christian experience. Our heavenly Father uses the various situations of life to bring us to a point of complete submission. His desire is not to break but to channel our will for His glory.

The opposite of meekness is also illustrated in the Scripture.

Paul speaks of those who are proud, boastful, sneering at God, disobedient to parents...hard headed...rough and cruel...betraying their friends, and puffed up with pride (2 Tim. 3, TLB).

Jude speaks of false teachers in the Early Church who reject and laugh at those in authority over them. They mock and curse at anything they do not understand, and do whatever they feel like. Jude says they follow the examples of Cain and Balaam, doing anything for money, and like Korah, they disobey God (Jude 3-11).

Although we may not fall into the categories of disobedience described by Paul and Jude, we do have a rebellious will and we need to understand that in the committed disciple, God desires to lead us into a life-style of meekness and full surrender.

4

BIBLE STUDY GUIDE

Today's Bible Reading: July 24/98
Rom. 13:1-2; 2 Tim. 3:1-4; Jude 1:8-11

1. What should the believer's attitude be towards authority? Rom. 13:1-2

Obedience to "Government" because they are not in Power without Gods Permission

2. What kind of attitude seems to be a growing problem in our world today? Draw a contrast between this and the biblical attitude of meekness and submission. 2 Tim. 3:1-4 *Difficult times People will be selfish greedy boastful conceited · insulting disobedient ungrateful irreligious · unkind merciless, slanderers treacherous - swollen with pride - The opposite to meekness & subm.*

3. Describe what Jude says about the false teachers who secretly slipped into the Early Church. Jude 1:8-11 *they despise Gods authority - They attacked with insults anything they didn't understand For the sake of money they were destroyed*

TODAY'S WORLD PRAYER EMPHASIS

LATIN AMERICA - SURINAME
- Population: 435,000
- Religion: Muslim 24% - Hindu 23.6:% - Non-religious/other 3% - Spiritist/animist 2.9% - Baha'i 1.2% - Christian 45.3%
- Needs:
  Suriname's post-independence experience has been disastrous. Pray for peace, godly leaders, stable government, economic improvement, and, above all, for spiritual awakening. The young nation is compartmentalized by race and religion, and the potential for further conflict remains.
  Pray for the less reached peoples: the Javanese, the Indian community, the Chinese, the Bush Negroes, the Guyanese refugees, and the Laotian Hmong. There are outreaches currently in place to reach these people, but many still have yet to hear the gospel.

Lesson 3
MEEKNESS MEANS HUMILTY & GENTLENESS

The second aspect of meekness has to do with how we relate to those around us. God is seeking to help us be humble, gentle, and kind, even to our enemies.

This does not mean that we are spineless or weak. Nor does it mean that we do not express our opinions.

What it does mean is that we serve and treat people with love and dignity. It means we do not strike back when others attack us or say evil about us.

The fact is, *it takes tremendous strength to be meek.*

Without the strength and power of the Holy Spirit, it's really impossible. Everything within our sinful nature seeks service and self-justification—to fight back, lash out, or get even.

The new nature of Christ within us, however, is the opposite. This new nature seeks to serve and to forgive others. It is gentle, even to those who hate us the most.

In using the word "meekness", Jesus was speaking of a type of submission that calls one to servanthood. In some cases, meekness may require the disciple to submit to serving the higher law of love instead of claiming his or her own rights.

In his book, *Matthew Henry's Commentary for Today's Reader, New Testament*, David Winter says, "The meek are those who are *gentle towards all men* (Tit. iii.2); who can bear provocation without being inflamed by it; are either silent, or return a soft answer; who can be cool when others are hot; and in their patience keep possession of their own souls, when they can scarcely keep possession of anything else.

"*They* are the meek, who are rarely and hardly provoked, but quickly and easily pacified; and who would rather forgive twenty injuries than revenge one, having the rule of their own spirits."

An attitude of meekness (submission to God, plus humility and gentleness to all people), allows God to empower our every ability, talent, and resource, and use it to His glory.

As a result, the meek inherit the earth. Literally, the world is ours (1 Cor. 3:21-23)!

6

BIBLE STUDY GUIDE

Today's Bible Reading:
Gal. 6:1; Eph. 4:2; Phil. 2:3; 1 Pet. 3:4

1. How are we to handle people who sin? Gal. 6:1 *gently reprove*
set him right - being careful
not to be tempted to sin
yourself.

2. How are Christians urged to treat one another? Eph. 4:2; Phil 2:3
Agree with each other in the Lord
humbly gently, patiently, humbly.
not boastful

3. What is one of the greatest inner-adornments a person can have? 1 Pet.
3:4 *Inner beauty - a gentle, quiet*
spirit

TODAY'S WORLD PRAYER EMPHASIS

EUROPE - SWEDEN
- Population: 8,326,000
- Religions: Non-religious/other 34.9% - Jews 0.19% - Muslim .0.8% - Protestant 60.4% - Roman Catholic 1.7% - Orthodox 1.3% - Marginal 0.64%
- Needs:
  Fifteen Swedish students have graduated from Crossroads School of Broadcasting. Pray that they will be affective in communicating the gospel.
  Pray for the growing evangelical minority among the pastors of the State Church.
  Pray for a spiritual outpouring in this nation. There are many nominal Christians who need a renewal of vision for the souls of their country.

Lesson 4

GROWING IN MEEKNESS

The character of God comes forth in the disciple's life in one of two ways.

The first is described in Romans 6:4-11. As a Christian you must count yourself dead to the old rebellious nature and alive unto God the Holy Spirit, who lives within you. (Much was said about how we yield to the Holy Spirit's control in book two of our *Life By Design* series.)

In each of us there are areas of sin and rebellion that we must deal with. According to the Scripture, we should, in faith, refuse to accept the pull of our old nature toward sin.

Our sinful nature will try to resist and always try to take us in the opposite direction. Yet we must count that old nature as dead in Christ and, instead, yield to the power of Christ that lives within us.

Therefore, meekness comes as we learn to surrender to truth and the nature of Christ.

The second way that God's character is brought forth in our lives is really simply an amplification of the first.

David, the psalmist, said, "Search me, O God, and know my heart;...see if there is any offensive way in me..." (Ps. 139:23-24).

Under the concept of spiritual mourning in *Life By Design—Book 2*, we discovered that God allows struggles to come into the lives of committed disciples.

Through these adverse circumstances, the Holy Spirit reveals things in our lives which do not conform to the image of Christ. As these things surface, the believer must learn to immediately count them as dead and surrender fully to the resurrection power of Christ within.

Meekness often comes as the result of God's dealings in our lives. As the carnal, rebellious nature is made powerless, a new, truly obedient nature begins to show forth in our attitude toward God and toward life in general.

When this occurs within us, we develop a thirst and a real openness to learn more about the things of Christ.

Our spirit becomes teachable and more submitted. And we are ever ready to be molded into the image of Christ so that we may be used by God in His service to others.

BIBLE STUDY GUIDE

Today's Bible Reading:
Rom. 6:12-14, 8:2; Psalm 139:23-24

1. How do we overcome the temptation to lash out, be unkind, and not be gentle with people? Rom. 6:12-14, 8:2 *Sin must not be your master - : The Law of the Spirit + Christ in us () has set us free -*

2. In what way can we ask God to show us where we need to be more gentle in our relationships? Psalm 139:23-24 *Ask the Lord To examine of thoughts & actions - Test us to see if we harbour evil thoughts - hindering our growth & ministry*

TODAY'S WORLD PRAYER EMPHASIS

EURASIA — TAJIKISTAN
- Population: 6,311,000
- Religions: Muslim 82.3% - Non-religious/other 13.2% - Jews 0.3% - Christian 4.2%- Protestant 0.04%
- Needs:
  Islamic fundamentalism, amply supported by Iranian propaganda and Afghan arms, could bring bigotry and other idealogical tyranny to the land. Pray for extremism to be restrained and Muslims to meet Christ.
  Pray for the conversion of Tajik and Uzbek leaders.
  Pray for the mountain peoples of the Pamirs in the east. In that region live six Ismaili Muslim peoples—the Ishkashimi, Roshani, Bartangi, Shughni, Wakhi, and Yazgulyam—who have never been reached with the gospel.

Lesson 5

A LIVING EXAMPLE

Colleen Townsend, in her book *A New Joy*, gives an excellent account of how God brings an attitude of meekness into the lives of those who would appear very unlikely to develop such an attitude.

It happened the night we met Hal. Just before we all sat down to dinner, there was a commotion at the door. It was a late and very noisy guest arriving. It was Hal. Obviously this wasn't his first party of the evening. Or perhaps he had had one all by himself before leaving home. Still, he was ready for conversation...in fact, he dominated it.

It was amazing how this man's presence seemed to fill the room. No doubt about it—here was a compelling, powerful personality. On the surface he was rough and loud, but as we were seated next to him for the rest of the evening, we began to see that the real man—the man underneath the scratchy surface—had great warmth, love, and sensitivity. We couldn't help thinking of the wonderful things God could do through such a man, if only...but Hal wasn't a Christian. He didn't seem to believe in anything but himself. Much as we coveted him for the Lord, we could only pray and wait.

Then, one Sunday a few weeks later, Hal and his whole family came to church—for the first time! I'm not sure why—perhaps out of curiosity...maybe a feeling of need. Anyway, it was just the beginning. In the months that followed, Hal stopped running his own life and turned it over to Christ.

Of course, I'm oversimplifying—it didn't happen that quickly. Nor did Hal give in easily. He struggled against submitting that powerful will to God—and at times he still struggles. From friends who knew him during his pre-Christian days, we learned that he was a man given to extremes. Some of this tendency remains—we see it cropping up every now and then—when he used to try to manipulate people into experiencing their faith in "the right way" (*his* way)...when he tried to link faith in Christ with a narrow political position. But always, because he is sincere in his commitment to Christ and puts Him before his own interests, he has abandoned these tactics. He has allowed himself to be led to where Christ is central to everything else in life. It's almost as if God had whispered to him, "You may be extreme in your love for Me, and in your love for your brothers and sisters in life, but nowhere else!"

Yes, Hal still struggles—but Jesus is a better, stronger, more persistent fighter! Now the real Hal has come to the surface where everyone can see him. He's a wonderful worker—not only in the church, but out in the community where his dynamic talents can do so much good. There seems to be no end to the things he can accomplish—but there is a difference in the way he uses his abilities. His strength—as great as ever—has been tamed. He uses it to lift up rather than to crush. Hal has gentle power.

Perhaps we must be strong before we can be gentle. It's a matter of learning how to use our muscles, spiritual as well as physical...the hand that strikes learning to shield...the tongue that wounds learning words of comfort...seeking out a person's needs so that we may help instead of attack....

■■

BIBLE STUDY GUIDE

Today's Bible Reading: Job 42:1-6

1. In Job 42, Job describes the change he has undergone in his thinking as a result of the trial God has allowed in his life. Relate in your own words the change Job indicates has happened. Job 42:1-6 *Job recognizises the awesomeness of Our All Powerful God. Now listens & Repent & follows with his heart Gods Desires instead of his own*

2. Using Job as an example, how do you think our struggles often make us more submitted to God's sovereignty or working in our lives? *When God allows impossible a difficult situations to be overcome in his strength we are becoming more mature in our Christian faith*

TODAY'S WORLD PRAYER EMPHASIS

PACIFIC — TONGA
- Population: 98,000
- Religion: Non-religious/other 0.1% - Baha'i 0.3% - Christian 99.6%
- Needs:

    Crossroads personnel have visited Tonga on two occasions. The king of Tonga is an evangelical Christian who desires that television in his county should be Christian television. Pray that this will happen.

    Pray for the growing Chinese community of immigrants from Hong Kong and China. These are the only unreached people group in Tonga.

    This last century has been one of spiritual decline with bitter schisms within the Christian community as well as the rapid growth of Mormons—now almost one-third of the population. Pray for the spirit of error to be bound and for the fragmented church to be united in revival.

WEEKEND DEVOTIONAL GUIDE

1. *Your prayer needs:* FOR - PAUL DAVID
HAMILTON GENERAL HOSPITAL
SHAUNA- HEALTH- STRENGTHEN HEART.
MIND SOUL - HEAL EMOTIONS
TOMMY- HEART FIBRILLATING
LOUISA - NEEDING WORK
DORIS- CRUCIAL- APPOINTMENTS
CHITTLEY -
OUR PASTOR - MEL -MINISTER- MEL
MIRIAM
ANDIRA & (all of the Lucias) JUDY ANDRE MARK

    • *Each week, write down your newest prayer requests.*
    •*After praying over them, transfer them to your main* God
Is Faithful Prayer List *on page 162. Remember them daily
in your prayers.*
    •*Each time a request is answered, draw a red line through
it and date it at the end.*

2. *Crossroads Christian Communications Prayer Need*

Pray for the children attending the Circle Square Ranches this summer, that many will find new life in Jesus Christ and return home with
a desire to serve the Lord.

3. *Lay Leadership International Prayer Need*

Pray for the daily outreach of *Life by Design* on the 100 Huntley Street
program. Pray for the many people who are involved, that their growth
in Christ will result in a greater outreach of love.

WEEKEND JOURNAL

Thoughts to reflect on and record:

1. As I begin this study on meekness, am I willing to let God change me in areas where I need to relate better to both Him and others around me? *YES*

2. Are there known areas of my will that are not fully submitted to certain authorities that God has placed over me? *YES*

3. Am I easily provoked? *NO* Am I cool when others are hot? *YES* Do I treat people with dignity and love? How much do I show forth the gentleness of Christ? *YES 2*

4. Can I recall any personal struggles that brought me to a greater level of submission to God?

5. What did the story of Hal, in lesson 5, say to me? *— HAVE A LISTENING HEART OPEN TO CALL OF JESUS - LEADING OF HOLY SPIRIT*

BEING MEEK BEFORE GOD

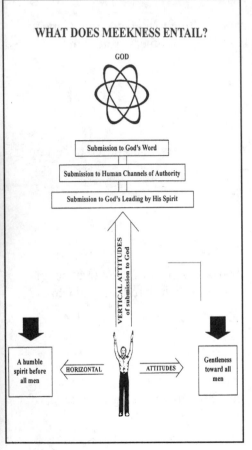

WHAT DOES MEEKNESS ENTAIL?

GOD

Submission to God's Word

Submission to Human Channels of Authority

Submission to God's Leading by His Spirit

VERTICAL ATTITUDES of submission to God

A humble spirit before all men

HORIZONTAL   ATTITUDES

Gentleness toward all men

The diagram in this lesson will appear numerous times in our daily studies of *"Blessed are the Meek."* In one glance it shows us what it means to be meek before God and others.

Let's take a brief look at what it means to be meek, or submitted to God.

As we grow in our relationship with Christ, the Holy Spirit is able to do a work in our lives. His primary work is to give us the knowledge and the power to be completely submissive to God through Jesus Christ.

This attitude of meekness toward the Lord will enable us to submit to His supreme Word on earth, to His human chains of authority, and to being led by His Holy Spirit.

One of the areas we struggle with the most is certain aspects of human authority.

Romans 13:1-2 says, "Everyone must submit himself to governing authorities, for there is no authority except that which God has established. The authorities that exist have been established by God. Consequently he who rebels against the authority is rebelling against what God has instituted...."

Of course there are times when authorities in our lives come into conflict with God's higher law or they become abusive and violate justice and love. These are special times when Christians are forced to serve the higher law of God's Word.

Nevertheless, as a general rule, meek people obey the various authorities God has placed in their lives. For as they submit to these human authorities, they are in essence submitting to God.

GOD
HUSBAND
GOVERNMENT

BIBLE STUDY GUIDE
Today's Bible Reading:
Matt. 22:29; Acts 4:18-19; Rom. 13:1-7; Titus 3:1

1. Why did Jesus say that even the religious leaders of His day were in error? Matt. 22:29 *— They did not Know the Scriptures of the Power of God*

2. What did Titus say about human chains of authority? Titus 3:1 *Obey rulers & authorities & be ready to be good in every way.*

3. As God's children, how are we to follow authority? Rom. 13:1-7 *God declares — Be obedient to State Authority*

4. Who did the Apostles recognize as the Higher Authority? Acts 4:18-19 *GOD — MESSIAH*

TODAY'S WORLD PRAYER EMPHASIS
EURASIA - TURKMENISTAN
- Population: 4,039,000
- Religion: Non-religious/other 18.2% - Muslim 76% - Christian 5.7% - Protestant .01% - Jewish .07%
- Needs:
  Turkmenistan is still not fully open to the gospel. Pray that there may be full religious freedom and opportunity for people to hear the gospel.
  Christians are few and mainly Russian, Ukrainian, or Armenian. Their numbers are decreasing through emigration. Pray that the few evangelical believers may be more free to witness and reach out to the unevangelized majority. There is only a handful of Turkmen believers known.

Lesson 7

GOD'S AUTHORITIES IN LIFE

In our last lesson, you were introduced to a basic diagram that shows the various aspects of meekness in a disciple's life. Today we continue looking at how meekness entails an upward, vertical submission to God.

There are basically three areas of authority in a Christian's life: God's Word, human authority, and the leading of the Holy Spirit. In this lesson, we discuss how they interelate. In other words, when human authority tries to usurp God's Word, or Christians usurp human authority just on the basis of what they "feel" is an inner leading of the Spirit, the higher authority—i.e., God's Word or the human authority He has established—must be obeyed.

The highest authority in the Christian's life is the Word of God. God's Word must become the supreme rule of faith and practice for every disciple. You must learn how to interpret it correctly, how to search out its principles, and how to submit to them in every life situation. Through careful study, you must come to know the Word thoroughly so that you can scrutinize every philosophy and practice in the light of the Scriptures (2 Tim. 2:15, 3:16-17).

The next authority in the Christian's life is human authority. All authority that exists has been ordained by God (Ro. 13:1). The disciple is obeying God's authority when he or she obeys any authority God has instituted. This includes authorities in the world, the home, and the church (Ro. 13:1-2; Eph. 5:23-24; Heb. 13:17).

Sometimes human authorities may come into conflict with the higher authority of God's Word. If they do, the disciple has no choice but to obey the Word of God. Meekness, however, implies that no retaliation be taken against human authorities who persecute the disciple because of his or her firm allegiance to God's supreme Word on earth (Acts 5:27-29).

The other authority in the Christian's life is the leading of the Holy Spirit. Discipleship involves a sensitivity to the leading of God's Spirit. This must also include the application of biblical principles that test the inner voice of the Spirit (1 Jn. 4:1-2).

You should never allow something which you feel as a leading from God's Spirit to usurp human authority. You must instead pray for creative alternatives, or else, a change of mind or the removal of the human authorities that are hindering your efforts to follow the leading of God's Spirit. In doing so, you submit yourself to the sovereignty and timing of God in your life. You allow Him to work out circumstances for you.

The disciple must be careful to discern which authority he or she must follow at any given time. Although the "ground-rules" have been laid, these

Shauna Margaret (handwritten)

are no substitute for praying and seeking guidance from God through His
Word and His Spirit.

■■■■■■■■■■■■■■■■■■■■■■■■■■■■■■■■■■■■

BIBLE STUDY GUIDE

30/7/98 (handwritten)

Today's Bible Reading:

Ro. 13:1-2; Eph. 5:22-6:3; Heb. 13:7,17; 2 Tim. 2:13, 3:15-16; 1 Jn. 4:1

1. Why are the Scriptures so important to us as we progress through life? 2
Tim. 3:15-16 *They are a pathway, straight & narrow Scriptures (inspired by God - truth rebuking error, correcting fault, instruction for righteousness)*

2. What must we seek and learn to do in relation to God's Word? 2 Tim.
2:15 *Learn to correctly teach the Word of God -*

3. Name three types of human authorities in our lives. Ro. 13:1-2; Eph.
5:22-6:3; Heb. 13:7, 17 *State - Husbands - Parents God's Word thru Study) Leaders*

4. What are we to do with regard to the leading of the Holy Spirit? 1 Jn. 4:1
Pray for discernment that that who claim to have the Holy Spirit are genuine.

TODAY'S WORLD PRAYER EMPHASIS

PACIFIC - TUVALU
- Population: 9,900
- Religion: Baha'i 3.4% - Protestant 93.8% - Roman Catholic 1.1%
- Needs:
  Tuvalu may be the first nation to disappear as a result of global warming and the rise
  in the level of the oceans. Pray that the uncertaintly of the future may bring
  spiritual earnestness.
  The Tuvalu Church is, in effect, the established church; nominalism and tradition
  are brakes on spiritual life and fervor. The new work of the Assemblies of God
  and Church of God of Prophecy are the only distinctly evangelical ministries on
  the islands. Pray for the spiritual life for all groups.

Lesson 8

BEING MEEK BEFORE PEOPLE

In the last few lessons we have looked at the first area of meekness which involves the Christian's vertical or upward submission to God through the various authorities He has ordained in the world.

In this lesson, we look at the second area of meekness which involves the Christian's horizontal or outward relationships with others. Christ calls us to a life of humility, gentleness, and non-retaliation.

Within the Church, Jesus Christ has given various abilities and talents, and assigned various responsibilities and roles to each individual member. Every member of the body of Christ has equal access and worth to God. As a result, we should never flaunt our position or area of ministry, no matter how prominent it may be within the body. If we boast of our position, we are succumbing to the "pride of life" that is one of the essential facets of worldliness mentioned in 1 John 2:15-16. Though He was great, Jesus Christ humbled Himself to fulfill the Father's will and took a place of no reputation. Likewise, all the members of Christ's body, regardless of their position, must constantly humble themselves before God and esteem all others higher than themselves (Phil. 2:3-4).

We also demonstrate the Spirit of Christ when we give a gentle answer to inflaming and provoking words, when we love our enemies, when we forgive seventy times seven, when we turn the other cheek, and when we go the second mile. Indeed, meekness produces a gentleness toward all people.

This gentleness toward all people is not spinelessness or denial of our submission to God's supreme Word on earth. It is, instead, how we react to those who oppose us and spitefully use us. We must always respond, not by demanding our own rights, but by demonstrating the higher law of Christ's love (Mt. 5:38-42).

Although humbling ourselves and being gentle toward others is a form of submission, it is also a form of liberation. As Richard Foster comments in his book *Celebration of Discipline*:

> It is the ability to lay down the terrible burden of always needing to get our own way. The obsession to demand that things go the way we want them to go is one of the greatest bondages in human society today....
>
> In the Discipline of submission we are released to drop the matter, to forget it....
>
> If you will watch these things you will see, for example, that almost all church fights and splits occur because people do not have the freedom to give in to each other....
>
> Do you know what a liberation it is to give up your rights?....It means freedom to obey Jesus' command, 'Love your enemies and pray for those

18

who persecute you' (Mt. 5:44).

To be gentle and humble is not only a sign of meekness, but it is a sign of a submissive spirit that lives in the freedom that comes from following the laws of Christ.

■■■■■■■■■■■■■■■■■■■■■■■■■■■■■■■■■■■■■■■

BIBLE STUDY GUIDE

Today's Bible Reading:

Lk. 6:27-31; Jn. 13:12-17; Phil. 2:8

1. Describe how, in a spirit and attitude of meekness and humility, Christ considered serving every person—rich or poor—before He considered serving Himself. Phil. 2:8 *He was humble a walked the Path of Obedience till the end.*

2. What lesson was Jesus trying to teach the disciples about the importance of every person to God, regardless of their position in society or how far down the social scale they exist? Jn. 13:12-17 *No Slave was greater or lesser than his master, teacher He set the example for all of us to follow*

3. What does it mean to be meek towards your enemies? Lk. 6:27-31 *Love, Bless, Pray for those who hate Curse do you harm. Be a Giver Do onto others as ---*

TODAY'S PRAYER EMPHASIS

EURASIA - UKRAINE
- Population: 53,770,000
- Religion: Non-religious 25.5% - Muslim 0.47% - Jewish 0.94% - Protestant 3.2% Catholic 15% - Orthodox 55% - Other 0.21%
- Needs:

    Mobile television production equipment, originally donated by Crossroads supporters for use in Western Europe, is now in use in Ukraine. Pray that many will be reached by the gospel through this venture.

    Pray that full religious freedom for all groups may be enshrined in the constitution, and that Christians may guard and make full use of that freedom.

    Pray for the missionaries to the Ukraine that the might reach the unreached or hard to reach peoples—middle class and educated; students; Crimean Tatars; and Ukrainian Jews.

Lesson 9
A GREAT LEADER WHO BECAME MEEK

In lesson two we looked at the original meaning of the Greek word for meekness. We discovered that like the breaking of a wild horse to the master's reins, God often uses circumstantial discipline to, in a sense, break us to His reign.

In this lesson we will discuss one of the most outstanding examples of this process: Moses.

Moses is the only man in the Bible, besides Jesus Christ, to be called meek. However, this meekness was not originally a "part of Moses' nature." Three particular instances in Moses' life show us that Moses' aggressive will needed to be channeled in a different direction.

The first instance came early in Moses' life when his undisciplined nature resulted in his committing murder (Ex. 2:12).

Later in his life, Moses was overcome by his anger at the unfaithfulness of the children of Israel which caused him to destroy the two tablets on which God had written the Ten Commandments at Mt. Sinai (Ex. 32:19).

Finally, Moses again lost his temper and disobeyed God by striking the rock twice for water instead of simply speaking to it as God had commanded (Nu. 20:11). This act of disobedience carried a great price—Moses would not be allowed to enter the Promised Land. *Consequence*

Yet for all of his mistakes, Moses was still called meek. Unlike any other biblical leader, he led a rebellious people, yet he himself constantly displayed an attitude of submissive obedience to God (Nu. 14:2-4, 11:13, 19).

In his youth, Moses was controlled by a raging sense of justice, and he struck out at those who, in his opinion, were acting unjustly. This streak of uncontrollable aggression was detrimental to him. And although Moses was a natural leader, God could not use him until that rebellious self-will had been disciplined, turned in a different direction, and brought into complete submission.

God used adversity to tame Moses, placing this great leader in the desert to herd sheep for 40 years. As a result of probably struggling for these years with feelings of worthlessness, Moses became a meek man. With his attitude of meekness, God was able to use Moses to fulfill His will.

Just as God used trials to bring Moses to a place of meekness, God also uses our struggles to discipline and remold us into people who are meek and gentle toward God and others.

As we grow in this attitude, we become more useful to God and reflect more of Christ's character to the world.

BIBLE STUDY GUIDE

Today's Bible Reading:
Exodus 2:11-12; 4:10-13; 6:6-12, 28-30; 7:10

1. What did Moses do as a young leader that showed he was anything but meek? Ex. 2:11-12 *He killed the one who killed the Hebrew*

2. After 40 years in the desert, does Moses appear to be the strong, confident leader we know he became? Ex. 4:10-13 *He was still feeling somewhat worthless but thru God all things are possible*

3. Even though Moses constantly lacked self-confidence and the Israelites refused to believe him, what made him strong? Ex. 6:6-12, 28-30; 7:10 *Ever increasing faith in the Lord - God thru Moses triumphed - Moses messenger of Gods Promises*

TODAY'S PRAYER EMPHASIS

EUROPE - UNITED KINGDOM
- Population: 58,210,000
- Religion: Non-religious 28% - Muslim 2.5% - Protestant 53.2% - Catholic .10% - Other 2.46%
- Needs:

  Strident propaganda of New Age and eastern mystical cults has eroded the Judeo-Christian heritage to the point that public opinion is no longer Christian. Religious pluralization has sapped the confidence of many Christans to testify boldly and even believe that Jesus Christ is the *only* way to the Father. Revival is needed once more. Pray for a greater prayer burden to unite Christians to seek that blessing.

  Pray for the local, Irish, and British politicians and church leaders who must tactfully and sensitively work toward a solution to the tragic cycle of violence, revenge, and communal fears brought about by the situation in Northern Ireland. Pray also for the numerous families who have lost members to the terrorist violence.

21

Lesson 10

THE MAKING OF PAUL

A nother fine example of someone who had to be disciplined and pre-pared for service to the Lord is the apostle Paul. Even after Paul be-came a disciple of Christ, his personality remained extremely aggressive. God worked to remold Paul for at least 11 or 12 years before he entered active ministry: 3 years in Arabia (Gal. 1:15-18) and 8 or 9 years making tents in Tarsus (Acts 9:30, 11:25-26).

In his book, *The Life of St. Paul*, James Stalker writes:

> Paul was now in possession of his gospel and was aware that it was to be the mission of his life to preach it to the Gentiles; but he had still to wait a long time before his peculiar career commenced. We hear scarcely anything of him for another seven or eight years; and yet we can only guess what may have been the reasons of Providence for imposing on His servant so long a time of waiting.
>
> There may have been personal reasons, for it connected with Paul's own spiritual history; because waiting is a common instrument of providential discipline for those to whom exceptional work has been appointed. A public reason may have been that he was too obnoxious to the Jewish authorities to be tolerated yet in those scenes where Christian activity commanded any notice. He had attempted to preach in Damascus, where his conversion had taken place, but was immediately forced to flee from the fury of the Jews; and, going thence to Jerusalem and beginning to testify as a Christian, he found the place in two or three weeks too hot to hold him. No wonder; how could the Jews be expected to allow the man who had so lately been the chief champion of their religion to preach the faith which they had employed him to destroy? When he fled from Jerusalem he bent his steps to his native Tarsus, where for years he remained in obscurity. No doubt he testified for Christ there to his own family, and there are some indications that he carried on evangelistic operations in his native province of Cilicia; but, if he did so, his work may be said to have been that of a man in hiding, for it was not in the central or even in a visible stream of the new religious movement.

After his years in Arabia, learning from God his special revelation for the Church, Paul returned to Jerusalem. Here he caused such an uproar among the Jews that the Church leaders, for fear of exciting more persecution than necessary, sent Paul back to Tarsus.

It must have been extremely difficult for Paul to learn God's patience and understand His purpose during the 9 years that followed. He had received God's special revelation, more than any other human had ever received, yet he sat making tents for 9 long years. During those years, however, God was reshaping Paul into a person of meekness.

In our modern world, a person of Paul's influence is often given evangelistic prominence almost immediately after conversion.) This, however, is very seldom God's way. His interest is in taking new believers and preparing them—discipling and equipping them—for future service. God works on His own time schedule, seeking to make each of us into meek servants who follow His will.

■■■■■■■■■■■■■■■■■■■■■■■■■■■■■■■■■■

BIBLE STUDY GUIDE
Today's Bible Reading: Acts 9:26-31, 11:19-26; Gal. 1:15-18

1. How many years after his conversion did Paul remain in Arabia? Gal. 1:15-18 _____ *3 yrs* _____

2. After Paul returned to Jerusalem from Arabia, what did the Apostles ask him to do? Acts 9:30 _____ *on to Tarsus* _____

3. After 8 or 9 years, who finally sought Paul out to help him in the ministry? Acts 11:25 _____ *Barnabas* _____

4. After his conversion, Paul immediately lost his high position in Judaism and then waited 11 years before entering the Christian ministry. How would you feel in similar circumstances? _____ *anxious to get on with Gods Purpose for him* _____

Continue to Pray for Andira

TODAY'S PRAYER EMPHASIS

LATIN AMERICA - URUGUAY
- Population: 3,246,000
- Religion: Non-religious 37.2% - Jewish .1.7% - Protestant 3.63% - Roman Catholic 48.3% - Orthodox O.93% - Other 3.5%
- Needs:
  Since 1986, the growth of some Pentecostal groups and Baptists has suddenly accelerated. Pray for this awakening to continue. ✓

  Lack of knowledge of God has given opening to a spirit of error. Brazilian spiritism has made a big impact on the country; there are now 1,200 registered occult centers. Pray for these delusions to be exposed and the demonic powers behind them to be defeated. ✓

WEEKEND DEVOTIONAL GUIDE

1. *Your prayer needs:* are for the Church a State Leaders
   Paul David -
   Shauna -
   Andrea & Family
   - Peg -

   Our Bible Study
   VBS. Teachers & Volunteers

• Each week, write down your newest prayer requests.
•After praying over them, transfer them to your main God
Is Faithful Prayer List *on page 162. Remember them daily
in your prayers.*
*•Each time a request is answered, draw a red line through
it and date it at the end.*

2. *Crossroads Christian Communications Prayer Need*

Pray that many people will come to visit the Crossroads Centre this
summer, and that they may be blessed and refreshed by the work of the
Lord in this place.

3. *Lay Leadership International Prayer Need*

Pray for the director, producer, and other production staff of the *Life
by Design* daily segments. Pray for the Holy Spirit's empowering as
each shooting takes place and as they are released over the TV air-
waves.

WEEKEND JOURNAL

Thoughts to reflect on and record:

1. What is my attitude towards government in general? Regardless of its failings, do I adhere to it as God's ordained authority in my life?

I believe I do

2. Do I respect the final authority of Scripture? Do I respect God's authority in the home and church? Do I seek to follow the authority of the Holy Spirit's leading?

With God's Help

3. Do I make a class distinction between wealthy or important people and those who have little? Do I serve the poor as quicly as I serve the rich?

Yes.

4. Am I open to being broken to the reign of God even more than I think I am presently?

I am.

5. If needed, am I willing to wait for the timing of the Lord and His preparation in my life regarding ministry as did Paul?

Yes.

OUR SUPREME EXAMPLE

Jesus Christ is our supreme example of meekness. He said, "Take my yoke upon you, and learn of me; for I am meek and lowly in heart..." (Mt. 11:29, KJV).

Christ did not possess a sinful, rebellious nature as we do. Thus, His character did not require training through the process of God's discipline and spiritual mourning in order to be meek. He did, however, face all the temptations that we face, yet He did not sin (Heb. 4:15).

Although His entire character exemplified meekness, there are three areas in particular that deserve our attention: His incarnation, His ministry, and His death.

The first example of the meekness of Christ is observed through the incarnation. Only perfect meekness would willingly lay aside all the glories of heaven and submit itself to the limitations of being born an ordinary human being while still remaining fully God (Phil. 2:5-8).

The second example of Christ's meekness can be found in His ministry, through which Jesus emphasized that He was fully submitted to God's will. The word He delivered was not His word, but the Father's (Jn. 7:16). The works He did were those which the Father had given Him to do (Jn. 5:19). The most important thing in His life was to meekly obey the will of the Father and to do His work (Jn. 4:34, 6:38).

The third and perhaps the greatest single display of meekness in Christ's life was His quiet acceptance of an unjust death at the hands of sinful people. He, who had created the universe and could call down more than 12 legions of angels to His rescue, meekly subjected Himself to a cruel death in order to accomplish the Father's plan to save the world (Isa. 53:7; 1 Pet. 2:21-24).

The most beautiful display of meekness throughout this horrible ordeal is seen when Christ prayed, "Father forgive them for they know not what they do" (Lk. 23:34, KJV). He readily forgave those who were administering to him so much pain and agony.

Indeed, Christ is our greatest example of meekness. In our struggle to reflect meekness that is pleasing to God, Jesus is our role model. He is our hope and our strength.

BIBLE STUDY GUIDE

Today's Bible Reading:
Matt. 26:50-54; Lk. 23:34-35; Jn. 4:34, 5:19, 6:38, 7:16-17

1. How was Christ completely submitted to God the Father? Jn. 4:34, 5:19, 6:38, 7:16-17 _It was time to Harvest. His_ _Through his total meekness of_ _Character he was able to_ _submit to his fathers plan for_ _mankind a Salvation plan_

2. Describe how Christ displayed meekness during His arrest and crucifixion Matt 26:50-54, Luke 23:34-35 _He cried_ _out to his father_ _Father forgive then for they_ _know not what they do_

TODAY'S WORLD PRAYER EMPHASIS

PACIFIC - VANUATU
- Population: 191,000
- Religion: Non-religious/other 1.2% - Animist and Cargo cultists 14.7% - Protestant 65% - Roman Catholic 16.2% - Marginal 2.91%
- Needs:
  Cargo cults and reversion to paganism have been major problems over the past 40 years. There are also many nominal Christians who follow "custom." Pray for decisive demonstrations of God's power among the largely traditional peoples of Tanna, Aniwa, Santo, and Vao.
  Bible translation is a major unfinished task. At least 8, and possibly 81, languages may require New Testament translations or revisions. Pray for wisdom as to which of the small language groups warrant the effort, and for translation teams of expatriates and nationals.

A QUICK GLANCE BACK

In this lesson we are going to quickly review what we have studied thus far about what it means to be meek.

First, we learned that meekness means that our rebellious self-will has been disciplined and brought into an attitude of total obedience to God.

Second, we saw that only as we surrender to the work of the Holy Spirit can meekness be produced in our lives.

Third, we discovered that we must cultivate three basic vertical attitudes toward God. These attitudes involve submission to God's Word, submission to human authority, and submission to the inner leading of God's Holy Spirit.

Fourth, we learned that we must cultivate an all-encompassing attitude of humility and gentleness toward all people. Cultivating such an attitude of meekness requires that we seek help from the Holy Spirit.

Fifth, we discovered that humility and gentleness does not mean weakness, spinelessness, or a compromising of our beliefs. It does, however, mean exhibiting a soft, loving reaction to others—even to those who oppose us and spitefully use us.

Sixth, we discussed how God made powerful, aggressive leaders like Moses and Paul into meek people who were totally submitted to Him. Only through discipline and redirection of their wills could they become useful servants of God.

Finally, we looked at Jesus Christ, the supreme example of meekness. Through His incarnation, His ministry, and His death, Christ teaches us what it truly means to be meek toward God and humble, gentle, and non-retaliatory toward people.

In the lessons ahead, we will explore further what is involved in being meek toward God and humanity.

BIBLE STUDY GUIDE

Today's Bible Reading:
Lk. 6:27-31; Ro. 8:14; 13:1-2; Eph. 5:22-6:3; Phil. 2:8; 2 Tim. 3:15-16; Heb. 13:7, 17; 1 Jn. 4:1

Today, review the following scriptures regarding meekness:

1. Submission to God's Word — 2 Tim. 3:15-16

2. Submission to human authorities — Ro. 13:1-2; Eph. 5:22-6:3; Heb. 13:7, 17

3. Submission to the Holy Spirit's leading — Ro. 8:14; 1 Jn. 4:1

4. Humility toward others — Phil. 2:8

5. Gentleness toward others — Lk. 6:27-31

TODAY'S WORLD PRAYER EMPHASIS

ASIA - VIETNAM
- Population: 75,030,000
- Religion: Non-religious/other 29.8% - Buddhist 52% - New Religions 5.2% - Muslim 0.2% - Animist 3% - Protestant - 0.8% - Roman Catholic 8.9% - Marginal 0.07%
- Needs:
  Vietnam remains one of the few avowed Communist nations in the world. Repression of religious, economic, and political freedoms continue. Pray that Vietnam might emerge from its suffering, be freed from past demonic and ideological bondages, and open for the gospel.
  In 1992, approximately 60 or more Christians were imprisoned for their faith. Pray for their witness in prison—many have come to know Christ because of this in the past. Pray also for these Christians' grieving, often destitute families.

OUR HIGHEST AUTHORITY

In this lesson, we begin a series of daily studies on what is involved in submission to the highest authority in our life—God's Word.

The Bible is our only infallible guide for faith. It is the foundation for what we believe and practice—how we live and serve God.

The Word of God helps build our character and direct our lifestyle. It should be our guide for all of our activities because it is to be the supreme authority in the life of all believers.

Christians have often faced persecution for holding to this truth. For example, the first Christians ran into stiff resistance from early Roman rulers. Roman law stated that all religion was tolerated as long as it recognized Caesar as the ultimate god and authority in their lives. It was this law that allowed the Jewish authorities to persuade the Romans to crucify Christ. And it was this law that caused many early believers to face great persecution and even death.

Since the Scriptures are our highest authority in faith and practice, we must interpret this book correctly and search out its principles and submit to them in every life situation. We must reject all philosophy or behavior that is contradictory to the written Word (2 Tim. 2:15, 3:16-17).

When discussing the interpretation of Scripture, Martin Luther, a great 16th century theologian, said:

> I have observed this, that all heresies and errors have originated, not from the simple words of Scripture...but from *neglecting* the simple words of Scripture and from the affection of purely subjective...tropes [figures of speech] and inferences.
>
> Each passage has one clear, definite, and true sense of its own. All others are but doubtful and uncertain opinions.[1]

Thus, it is important as Christians that we learn how to skillfully interpret and obey God's Word.

In the lessons ahead, we will look at the things that guide us as we study and meditate upon God's Word daily.

---

[1] Quoted in F.W. Farrar's *History of Interpretation* (Baker Book House, 1961 [1886]), p. 327.

BIBLE STUDY GUIDE

Today's Bible Reading:
2 Tim. 2:15; 2 Tim. 3:16-17

1. In order to obey the Scriptures, what must we do? 2 Tim. 2:15 *Do Your best to win approval in the sight of God - teaching correctly without leaving error from scriptures the Promises of Your Awesome God.*

2. How is the Word of God to be used? 2 Tim. 3:15-16 *to give us wisdom & lead us to Salvation*

TODAY'S WORLD PRAYER EMPHASIS

PACIFIC - WALLIS & FUTUNA ISLANDS
- Population: 16,000
- Religion: Non-religious/other 1.1% - Protestant 1.5% - Roman Catholic 97.4%
- Needs:

Pray for the outreaches to these islands. Until 1985 this territory was one of the few countries of the world without a congregation of evangelical believers. However, since then there has been growth, as well as persecution of the small outreaches.

The Catholic and Polynesian culture and social structures have become so interwoven that adherence to Christianity is often more outward than through a living, personal faith. Pray for first-hand faith for these two island peoples.

Many islanders have migrated to other areas seeking work. Pray that some may be won to a personal commitment to Christ there, and thus bring blessing to their homeland.

GOD'S INSPIRED WORD OF TRUTH

As we continue our study on the highest authority in a believer's life, let's look closer at why we believe the Bible is God's inspired Word.[1]

The Bible clearly claims to be God's inspired Word of truth to humankind (2 Tim. 3:16; 2 Pet. 1:20-21). The truth of this claim must be evaluated on the basis of the nature of the Bible's message itself, as well as the integrity and accuracy of those who recorded that message. Like most fundamental beliefs in life, believing that the Bible is the Word of God is the result of faith or trust. The Bible does not attempt to present arguments for its claim of inspiration, it simply says, "thus saith the Lord...."

Our belief by faith that the Bible is the inspired Word of God rests upon certain facts, particularly those related to Jesus Christ. These facts can be divided into five separate foundational truths we will call pillars.

PILLAR ONE — HISTORICAL ACCURACY —The historical accuracy of both the Old and New Testaments is constantly being affirmed by archaeological research.

PILLAR TWO — THE CLAIMS OF CHRIST —The claims that Jesus Christ made were: to be God (Jn. 10:30-33), to be Truth itself (Jn. 14:6), and to speak God's message (Jn. 7:16).

PILLAR THREE — THE PROMISES OF CHRIST —He promised to guide the disciples in recording His words (Jn. 14:26), and to speak through them (Lk. 10:16). He also promised that the disciples would be His witnesses with the help of the Holy Spirit (Jn. 15:26-27; Acts 1:8).

PILLAR FOUR — THE INTEGRITY OF CHRIST —The integrity of Jesus Christ gives us good reason to believe His claims are true. We see on one occasion that even when given the opportunity, Christ's enemies could not accuse Him of any sin (Jn. 8:46). In this same regard, we read that even Pontius Pilate, the one who condemned Christ to the cross, found Him not guilty (Lk. 23:4).

PILLAR FIVE — THE RESURRECTION OF CHRIST —The resurrection not only fulfilled Christ's own prophecies concerning Himself (Mk. 8:31, 9:31; Lk. 18:31-33), but it also vindicated His claim to be God and confirmed the truthfulness of His promises to the disciples concerning their record of His words and deeds which we call the New Testament.

Together, these five pillars give us a solid foundation for our belief in the inspiration of the Scripture.

[1]This lesson is taken from a previous lesson in *New Life Studies* , *Vol. 1* by James D. Craig (Lay Leadership International, 1992) pp. 43-45.

■■■■■■■■■■■■■■■■■■■■■■■■■■■■■■■■

BIBLE STUDY GUIDE

Today's Bible Reading:
Jn. 1:1-14; 1 Jn. 1:1-4; 2 Pet. 1:19-21

1. Who does "the Word of God" refer to, according to John 1:1, 2, & 14?

_____

_____

_____

_____

2. In giving the inspired written Word, who were the New Testament authors writing about? 1 Jn. 1:1-4 _____

_____

_____

3. According to Peter, how were the Scriptures created? 2 Pet. 1:19-21 ____

_____

_____

_____

TODAY'S WORLD PRAYER EMPHASIS

AFRICA - ZAMBIA
- Population: 10,174,000
- Religion: Non-religious 0.5% - Traditional 23% - Bahai' 0.3% - Muslim 1% - Protestant 27% - Roman Catholic 32% - Marginal 8% - Orthodox 0.04%
- Needs:
  Zambia currently has a Christian president. Pray that the leaders of the land may live out their faith and not use their power for personal gain or sectional interests.
  Pray that God will give a united vision to the Christian leaders as they tackle the many problems facing the nation.
  Pray that Christians may set the moral tone in a country racked with AIDS, and that they can minister to those dying of the terrible disease. Immorality is so widespread that new moral foundations must be laid.

BUILDING OUR CONFIDENCE

As we look further at what it means to be meek toward God, we continue exploring the highest authority in our lives—God's Word.

Today's lesson looks at evidence as to why the Bible is God's inspired message to His creation.[1]

Throughout history, the Bible, as God's message to humanity, has demonstrated a dynamic ability to change the lives of individuals, as well as produce social reform. In the personal experiences of countless thousands of believers, the promises of God's Word have been fulfilled.

Furthermore, it is logical to assume that if the Bible was God's Word, He would protect it from destruction so that future generations could hear its message. This has indeed been the case. At times in history people have sought to stamp out the Bible (e.g., the Diocletian Edict in A.D. 303 to burn all Bibles). But they have failed. This fulfills Christ's promise in Matthew 24:35 that "Heaven and earth will pass away, but my words will never pass away."

Finally, the Bible has accurately predicted many historical events. Only God could do this. For example, in Isaiah 11:11-12, the prophet proclaims that the Lord will gather His people from the four corners of the earth and re-establish them as a nation. In 1948, 3,000 to 4,000 years later, Israel did become an established nation with political boundaries.

A second example of the accuracy of the Bible comes through the various detailed predictions concerning the life of Christ. The prophet Micah foretold Bethlehem as the birthplace of Christ (Micah 5:2). The prophet Isaiah spoke of the nature of Christ's ministry and His crucifixion (Isa. 61:1-2; 53). The Psalmist and the prophet Zechariah also discuss His scourging and crucifixion (Ps. 22:18; Zech. 12:10). And finally, the Psalmist gives a beautiful picture of the resurrection (Ps. 16:9-11).

As disciples of Christ, we must first accept the Bible as God's Word and inspired message to us. Then we must learn how to properly understand and use His message. This aspect will be discussed in future lessons.

---

[1] This lesson is also taken from *New Life Studies, Vol. 1* by James D Craig (Lay Leadership International, 1992) pp. 45-46.

BIBLE STUDY GUIDE

Today's Bible Reading:
Matt. 24:35; Acts 2:22-28; Isa. 53:4-5; Micah 5:2; Psa. 16:9-11

1. What did Christ say about His Word? Mt. 24:35 *Heaven Earth shall pass away but my Word shall never pass away.*

2. What did each of the following scriptures accurately foretell?
a. Micah 5:2 *foretold that Jesus would rule Israel.*

b. Isaiah 53: 4-5 *Christs crucifixion*

c. Psalm 16:9-11 *A Promise for mankind for Eternal Life*

3. What Old Testament scripture did Peter confirm was a prophecy concerning Christ's resurrection? Acts 2:22-28 *Ps - 61:1-2*

TODAY'S WORLD PRAYER EMPHASIS

ASIA - AFGHANISTAN
- Population: 23,141,000
- Religion: Muslim 99% - Hindu 0.3% - Christian 0.01%
- Needs:

The devastation of war has brought incredible suffering to the nation, yet the people are more receptive to the gospel than ever. It will take decades to clear the mines and rebuild homes, schools, farms and lives. Pray for peace and deliverance from further tyrannies.

Afghanistan is one of the least reached lands in the world. There is not one single church building in a land of 48,000 mosques. Pray for the 88 tribes of unreached peoples in the land, especially the Pushtuns, the Uzbeks and Turkmen, the Tajiks, the Hazaua, the Kuchi, the Char Aimaq, and the Nuristani.

Afghan believers are few and mostly Dari-speaking. Their numbers have multiplied due to the witness of expatriates. Pray for the continuing growth and survival of this small but strong Church; the fundamentalist government could destroy it.

WEEKEND DEVOTIONAL GUIDE

1. *Your prayer needs:*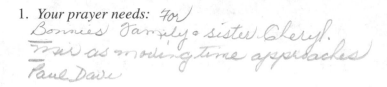

• *Each week write down your newest prayer request.*
• *After praying over them, transfer them to your main* God is Faithful *prayer list on page 162 and remember them daily.*
• *Each time a request is answered, draw a red line through it and date it at the end.*

2. *Crossroads Christian Communications Prayer Need*

Pray for God's continued guidance regarding the outreach of Crossroads USA, as the ministry seeks to reach more Americans for Christ than ever before.

3. *Lay Leadership International Prayer Need*

Pray for the LLI staff in the U.S. as they work with churches interested in discipleship, ship materials, and seek to see *Life by Design* released on stations across America.

WEEKEND JOURNAL

Thoughts to reflect on and record:

1. As I look to Jesus as my example, am I willing to take His yoke and let Him teach me both through His Word and life experiences how to be meek?

With the help of the Lord & Holy Spirit I do my utmost to please him

2. Lord, help me surrender to the inner work of your Holy Spirit and learn the ways of meekness as did Moses, Paul, and other great men and women of God.

Thank you Lord. yes I will

3. In a society where so many things oppose what God has said, am I willing to stand out, regardless, as one who lives under the supreme authority of God's Word.

yes   In thy Strength Lord

4. When I read the Bible, do I approach it as a very special inspired revelation from God? Do I see it as different from any other book?

Oh yes

5. Why do I personally believe it to be God's inspired Word to mankind?

Because he said it was.
God of Creation
God of light
to thee be the Glory

CORRECTLY INTERPRETING GOD'S WORD

In this lesson, we begin to learn how to interpret the Word of God. The chart presented here has been provided to aid us in our study.

The center column of the chart contains the key to correctly interpreting God's Word. Only the Holy Spirit can reveal God's truth to each one of us—student as well as teacher (1 Cor. 2:11-14). Jesus called Him "the Spirit of truth" and promised that He would come to dwell within us in order to teach us God's truth (Jn. 14:16-17,26).

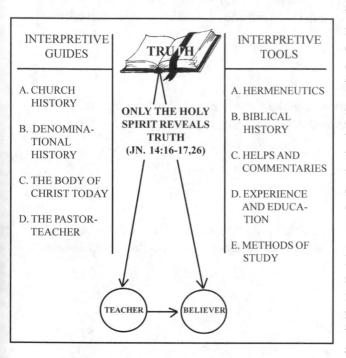

Referring to the Holy Spirit, John says that the anointing which we have received will teach us the truth of how to abide in Christ (1 Jn. 2:27). Believers must rely upon this teaching work of the Holy Spirit if they are to interpret God's Word correctly.

As you read the Bible and take time to reflect on what it says, the Holy Spirit illuminates it to your understanding. When you read the Bible and seek out its truths, something happens that is beyond ordinary learning and comprehension—the Holy Spirit makes the truth real. Often as you study a portion of scripture, certain words will almost leap out at you. Other times you will see a new truth in something you have read many times before. This also occurs as you hear or are taught God's Word. As the teacher, who has learned from the Holy Spirit, shows you a truth, the Holy Spirit also reveals it to you. If you are really listening, there will always be something that will minister to you. These situations are only a few examples of the Holy Spirit's illumination of the Word.

Even though the Holy Spirit is our true Illuminator and Teacher, God has set guidelines to help us be sure that what we are hearing is from the Holy Spirit. Because we are imperfect human beings, it is important that we test our thoughts against what the Holy Spirit has taught others throughout the course of history.

Interpreting Scripture is a learning process that involves not only our own private thoughts, but the testing of those thoughts against what other learned people have discovered as well, and testing everything against the foundational truths of God's Word when taken as a whole.

■■■■■■■■■■■■■■■■■■■■■■■■■■■■■■

BIBLE STUDY GUIDE
Today's Bible Reading:
Jn. 14:16-17, 26; 1 Cor. 2:9-14; 1 Jn. 2:27

1. Who is the person who teaches us God's Word? 1 Jn. 2:27; Jn. 14:16-17, 26 _God's Holy Spirit_

2. How does the believer comprehend, or understand, God's Word? 1 Cor. 2:9-14 _By testing our thoughts our understanding against scripture, Our Spirit tuned to the Spirit of God - Holy Spirit._

TODAY'S WORLD PRAYER EMPHASIS

MIDDLE EAST - ALGERIA
- Population: 29,306,000
- Religion: Non-religious/others 0.2% - Muslim 99.4% - Protestant 0.08% - Roman Catholic 0.32%
- Needs:
  Pray for God's ruling in the affairs of the people and government of this nation, that He may grant democratic moderation and religious freedom to the country. Algeria has become a political time bomb.
  The unreached comprise virtually the whole nation. Pray that God will pour out His Spirit on the growing cities, as well as the young people, the Berber peoples of the Atlas, the Tuareg, and the Mzab oasis towns in the Sahara.
  Pray that Christian media will survive in this internally restrictive nation. Pray especially for radio broadcasts, audio-visual ministries, and the ministry of Christian music through the distribution of cassette tapes.

GUIDING AUTHORITIES

There are certain authorities in believers' lives that guide them in what they believe the Holy Spirit is wanting to teach them through the Scriptures. These authorities are part of God's provision for helping Christians become mature in their faith so that they are not tossed to and fro by every wind of change in doctrines (Eph. 4:13-14).

Let's refer back to the left hand column of the diagram given in our last lesson. These authorities can be likened to college professors who gives you instruction as to where to dig out the truth. You have to go to the library and do the research, but your professor has given you guidance in finding the material you need. You then bring this material back to the professor for his or her verification in an essay or paper.

So it is with the guiding authorities in spiritual matters. You must be taught by the Holy Spirit's illumination. However, these guiding authorities help you find the truth and verify what you have discovered. They keep you on the right track.

The following authorities establish guidelines that help us interpret correctly what we think we hear God saying to us as we study His Word.

First, Christian doctrine has been clarified in church history through the controversies created by the appearance of various erroneous interpretations of the teachings of Scripture. The study of such errors in church history assists us in correctly interpreting the Scripture on the basis of knowing the pitfalls of the past.

Second, many denominations have arisen as a result of an emphasis on a particular aspect of doctrine that was being ignored by the Church as a whole. Their reassertion of a particular area of biblical truth and their teaching concerning that area of truth can assist all sincere students who seek to interpret God's Word correctly.

Third, the body of Christ today serves as a guideline against extreme error. Although there are various differences of belief, there still remains a basic agreement concerning the fundamentals of Christian doctrine among the vast majority of those today who regard the Bible as the Word of God. Those who claim to have some new revelation that God has never shown others in the body of Christ are in a position of grievous error.

Finally, according to Ephesians 4:11-14, God has placed in the church a pastor-teacher who is to be faithful above all else in preaching sound doctrine that will guide people as they seek to understand the Word of Truth (Titus 1:7-9, 2:1).

Therefore, we must not try to determine everything about truth on our own. It is very important that we seek out authorities to help us discover and verify truths that we find in God's Word.

■■■■■■■■■■■■■■■■■■■■■■■■■■■■■■■■■■■

BIBLE STUDY GUIDE
Today's Bible Reading:
Eph. 4:11-16; Titus 1:9-11

1. Who equips God's people for the work of the ministry? Eph. 4:11-12 ____
   CHRIST

2. What happens when people are fully equipped? Eph. 4:13-14 ____
   We have power & armour to do our ministry for Christ God thru Holy Spirit.

3. What does a good pastor do? Titus 1:9 *Hold firm to the truth of the scripture. Be our Shepherd in whom we can put our trust*

TODAY'S WORLD PRAYER EMPHASIS

EUROPE - BOSNIA & HERCEGOVINA
- Population: 4,422,000
- Religion: Muslim 40% - Non-religious/other 18% - Protestant 0.04% -Roman Catholic 14% - Orthodox 27.9% - Marginal 0.02%
- Needs:

  Pray that the war in this nation will come to a peaceful end, and that the Lord would do a miracle of healing and reconciliation among the people of the nation.

  Currently two Bosnians are studying at the school of broadcasting in Burlington. They have an open door for broadcasting the gospel when they return. Pray their ministry will be effective.

  Bosnian Muslims are the least reached people group in all of Europe. Christianity is seen as partly to blame for their agony—Serbs being Orthodox and Croats Catholic. Pray for Christians to be called to minister to the needs of these people in Bosnia and in all of the countries to which they have fled.

GUIDING HELPS

As we continue our study concerning the interpretation of Scripture, we want to refer back once again to the left column of the diagram on page 38. With this lesson, we will begin discussing the science of how to correctly interpret the Bible. This is called *hermeneutics*.

Author F.W. Farrar, in his book *History of Interpretation*, outlines these principles by quoting Martin Luther. He says, "Luther, in his preface to Isaiah (1528) and in other parts of his writings, lays down what he conceives to be the true rules of Scripture interpretation. He insists (1) on the necessity for grammatical knowledge; (2) on the importance of taking into consideration times, circumstances, and conditions; (3) on the observance of the context; (4) on the need of faith and spiritual illumination; (5) on keeping what he called 'the proportion of faith'; and (6) on the reference of all Scripture to Christ."

This, however, is only a brief example of what the science of interpretation (*hermeneutics*) entails. The following are some suggested helps in the process of interpretation.

First, biblical history gives us an understanding of the plan of God for the ages and the overall flow of the Bible's message.

It can also provide background material which is invaluable to the understanding of Scripture. This is particularly true for the historical and prophetic books of the Old Testament, the Gospels, and the Book of Acts.

Second, helps and commentaries serve as effective guides and checks in regard to our own interpretation. They can also give insights into the meaning of the text, based upon the author's study of Scripture in the original languages.

Helps and commentaries should only be used to *supplement* our own personal study of the Scripture. And they are definitely not a substitute for the Word of God.

Finally, our experience and our educational background can also serve to enhance our understanding of various biblical truths. These, however, are no substitute for the illumination of the Holy Spirit. All human wisdom must subject itself to the supreme authority of God's Word. Any knowledge that denies or is contrary to the claims of Scripture must be rejected.

Just as there are guiding authorities to help us as the Holy Spirit illuminates truth to our minds, so there are also many other helps along the way as we grow and mature in our faith. To once again review these authorities, you can return to our diagram on page 38 in lesson 16.

BIBLE STUDY GUIDE

Today's Bible Reading:
1 Tim. 2:15; 2 Tim. 3:16-17; 2 Pet. 1:20-21; 1 Jn. 1:1-4

Today, reflect on some of the scriptures we have studied thus far regarding the authority of God's Word.

_____

_____

_____

_____

_____

_____

_____

_____

_____

_____

_____

_____

_____

TODAY'S WORLD PRAYER EMPHASIS

MIDDLE EAST - BAHRAIN
- Population: 601,000
- Religion: Non-religious/other 1.5% - Muslim 85% - Hindu 6.2% - Protestant 1.5% - Orthodox 1.3% - Roman Catholic 4.5%
- Needs:
  This nation has provided a good base for Christian witness since the beginning of the century. There is opportunity for witnessing through the multi-national Christian expatriate community. Pray that individuals may have the courage and wisdom to actually do so beyond their own cultural group.

  Pray especially for the one Arabic-speaking evangelical congregation (made up mainly of expatriates) and for their witness to the many Muslims who have never been exposed to the gospel.

  Pray also for the few national believers who meet privately in their homes.

HOW TO STUDY GOD'S WORD

P robably the most important guiding help is to know *how* to study God's
Word. In this lesson we will discuss different methods that are very
helpful when studying the Bible for understanding.

There are various ways to approach the study of the Scriptures. Their
combined use can enhance our total understanding of the Bible's message.
The following are some examples of these approaches.

1.   *Scripture Memorization*
      This study method involves committing to memory key passages of
      Scripture, particularly those that are helpful in our daily walk with
      the Lord.

2.   *Topical Study*
      This involves collecting information from a number of different
      passages of Scripture that all relate to a single topic; such as the
      prayer life of Christ, repentance, faith, stewardship and so forth.

3.   *Inductive Bible Study*
      Inductive Bible Study involves carefully studying a selected pas-
      sage in depth. It usually has three steps: observation, interpreta-
      tion, and application.

4.   *Overview and Outline*
      This involves surveying an entire section of Scripture, such as a
      complete book of the Bible, in order to prepare a detailed outline of
      its contents.

5.   *Biographical Studies*
      This is a specialized form of topical study where all references re-
      lating to one individual are studied in order to learn spiritual lessons
      from that person's life.

6.   *Biblical Typology*
      This is an older form of study that relates to discovering divinely
      ordained symbols of New Testament truth contained in the Old Tes-
      tament. An example would be the study of the tabernacle to see
      how its construction and articles portray several important facts
      about Jesus Christ.

7.   *Expository Study*
      This method is very comprehensive and searches in all directions for

any information that is necessary to "exposit" or "bring out" the meaning of the text.

Each of these different studies has advantages and disadvantages. It is often best to try them all and find the one that works best for you on a daily basis. However, do not limit yourself to one form of study. Each method helps to discover truths in Scripture.

■■■■■■■■■■■■■■■■■■■■■■■■■■■■■■■■■

BIBLE STUDY GUIDE
Today's Bible Reading: Psalm 23

Today we begin a two-part study that will introduce you to meditating on and prayerfully studying the Scripture for yourself. We have chosen Psalm 23 to use in this study. We begin by looking at each phrase in each verse. The following questions are similar to the type of questions you might ask yourself as you meditate on other scriptures in the future. Write down your answer to each question on a separate sheet of paper.

1. Who is the shepherd in verse 1?
2. What does the shepherd do? (v. 1)
3. What does it mean to not be in want?
4. What does laying down and green pastures symbolize to you? (v. 2)
5. Picture yourself beside still quiet waters. Relate that to what you see your Shepherd, Christ, doing for you. (v. 2)
6. When your mind or soul is tested, what does the shepherd do? (v. 3)

TODAY'S WORLD PRAYER EMPHASIS

AFRICA - BENIN
- Population: 5,573,000
- Religion: Tribal religions 54.8% - Muslim 17% - Protestant 4% - Roman Catholic 21.7% - Marginal 2.47%
- Needs:
  Church growth is a new phenomenon. Pray for the raising up of more leaders; pastoral training; and the vision for reaching the unreached people and the strategy to implement it.
  Pray for the unreached peoples, especially the Fon, the Muslims, and the 800,000 urbanites. Pray also for those in the Togo border strip, the middle strip where there are no indigenous churches, and the southwest corner.

ANOTHER GLANCE BACK

Before we move on to section two to look at other areas of meekness toward God, let's briefly glance back at what we have learned about submitting to God's Word—the highest authority in a believer's life. We are doing this because it is so very important that we remember the truths presented in these lessons.

First, we discovered that the Bible is the only infallible guide to a believer's faith (what one believes) and practices (how one lives and serves God—including one's character, lifestyle, and activities.)

Second, we studied the importance of accepting the Bible as God's holy and inspired Word to humanity. It was supernaturally given, and has been protected by God through the ages so that every generation may learn its truths.

Finally, we discovered that even though the Holy Spirit is our real Teacher—the One who illuminates or makes the truth in God's Word real to our minds—we must be careful to surround this very personal daily experience with certain guiding authorities and tools which will help show us how to understand God's Word correctly.

For example, we discussed the fact that Church history, denominational history, the body of Christ today, and the ministry of the pastor-teacher can help guide us in our understanding of what God is saying.

We also learned that interpretive tools, such as the principles of hermeneutics, various methods of study, biblical history, and commentaries, as well as our own education and experience, can also assist us in understanding God's Word.[1]

It is important to the Christian to understand God's Word. As the ultimate authority in his or her life, the Christian must understand the Bible in order to obey its precepts and continue to grow and mature in his or her faith and practice.

---

[1]Further information on the personal, in-depth study of Scripture can be found in the third chapter of *New Life Studies, Vol. 1*, available through Lay Leadership International. There are also a large number of other helpful books available by various authors at your local library or Christian bookstore.

BIBLE STUDY GUIDE

Today's Bible Reading:
Psalm 23

Today we continue to learn how to meditate upon and prayfully study God's Word. We begin in Psalm 23:3.

1. Where does the shepherd guide you, and for what purpose? v. 3
2. When facing danger, or even death, how can the Lord help you? v. 4
3. What symbol does the writer use to depict God's discipline and correction?
4. Spend time meditating upon verses 5 and 6. Ask yourself similar questions as you learn more about ways to literally *feed* on God's Word. Write your thoughts on a separate sheet of paper.

TODAY'S WORLD PRAYER EMPHASIS

CARIBBEAN - BRITISH VIRGIN ISLANDS
- Population: 12,950
- Religion: Non-religious/other 2.9% - Baha'i 0.9% - Hindu 0.34% - Muslim 0.31% - Protestant 86.5% - Roman Catholic 6.3% - Marginal 2.7%
- Needs:
  The tourist trade brings large numbers of people seeking fun. Yet most of their lives are empty without Christ. Pray that local believers may be a good testimony to them.

  Pray for revival and for Christian families to live exemplary lives. The beauty of the islands belies the spiritual need. There are many churches, and most people profess to be Christians, yet sin mars the lives of many. More than three-quarters of all births are illegitimate.

WEEKEND DEVOTIONAL GUIDE

1. *Your prayer needs:*

• *Each week write down your newest prayer requests.*
• *After praying over them, transfer them to your main* God is Faithful
Prayer List *on page 162 and remember them daily.*
• *Each time a request is answered, draw a red line through it and date it
at the end.*

2. *Crossroads Christian Communications Prayer Need*

Pray that many people will continue to be reached through the *100
Huntley Street* daily television ministry. Pray those who watch who
are not Christians will come to a saving knowledge of our Lord Jesus
Christ.

3. *Lay Leadership International Prayer Need*

Pray for Don Hill as he gives leadership to the LLI Discipleship and
Life by Design ministry. Pray that God will give him great wisdom
and that the Lord's perfect will will be accomplished.

WEEKEND JOURNAL

Thoughts to reflect on and record:

1. Do I take time to meditate upon the Scriptures, in addition to reading a portion every day? Do I stop and meditate upon one or two key scripture verses and let the Holy Spirit illuminate them directly to my heart and mind?

2. Do I see the value of sound doctrine? Do I weigh everything I am taught against the teaching of my church, pastor, and the general body of Christ?

3. Do I use a commentary and other readily available helps to guide me in my reading of the Scriptures? Do I see it as important enough to invest in one or more of these guiding helps?

4. Do I actually take time to study God's Word, using a proven method of Bible study?

5. Lord, teach me Your ways. May the Holy Spirit illuminate Your Word as I take time to read and study it. Help me to listen closely to those who labor in Your Word and doctrine, realizing that they have a responsibility to watch over my soul and keep me from error. Amen.

Section II:

Understanding Meekness in Human Authority & the Leading of God's Spirit

Experience has long proven that no one is an island. As long as there is life, we will continually affect one another. Hence, there has always been a need for order and rules to govern how we behave toward each other.

God, who designed us in such a social fashion, has accordingly delegated certain areas of His authority to human representatives. Meekness means obeying those who have been given the right to lead us in the home, the church, and all other matters pertaining to society.

For the believer, there is yet another dimension of our Father's rulership—the still small inner voice of the Holy Spirit. This proves difficult at times as we seek to obey what we sense God is saying and balance it against the will of those He has placed in authority over us.

51

RELATING TO HUMAN AUTHORITY

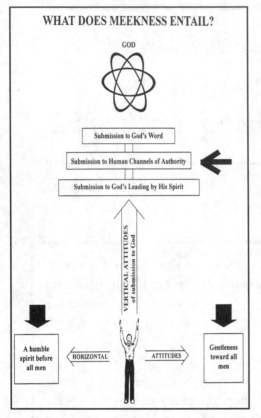

WHAT DOES MEEKNESS ENTAIL?

GOD

Submission to God's Word

Submission to Human Channels of Authority

Submission to God's Leading by His Spirit

VERTICAL ATTITUDES
of submission to God

A humble spirit before all men

HORIZONTAL   ATTITUDES

Gentleness toward all men

In the first section we looked at what it means to be meek and live under the highest authority in a believer's life—God's Word. In this section, we will focus on the second level—God's human channels of authority.

Many Christians fail to recognize that when they submit to the various institutions of human authority that they are actually submitting to God (Titus 3:1-3; 1 Pet. 2:12-15). True discipleship requires a renewed and biblical understanding of this fact.

The modern disciplines of social science often promote the concept that humans are created to be highly individualistic. Unfortunately, this is often unbalanced and contributes to a breakdown of effectiveness in many Christian ministries today. For this reason, we need to understand what it means to be submitted to God's channels of authority in the world, the home, and the church.

Jude warns the church about those who creep in unnoticed, those who reject authority and revile angelic majesties (Jude 8-9). As the Scripture says, "Even the archangel Michael, when he was disputing with the devil about the body of Moses, did not dare to bring slanderous accusation against him, but said, 'the Lord rebuke you!'" (Jude 9). Michael would not deal directly with the authority given to Lucifer. He had to leave him to God's judgment alone.

Even the Lord Jesus Christ respected the laws of His time. For example, He respected the authority of those in charge of the Temple and paid the half-shekel tax (Mt. 17:24-27). Jesus knew the authorities of His day were spiritually bankrupt. Nevertheless, He still told the people to submit to the authority of the scribes and the Pharisees as the recognized teachers of the law (Mt. 23:1-3).

We are not called to be rebellious people. We are called to submit to human authority, for it has been established by God. When we obey human authority we are really obeying God (Ro. 13:1-2).

■■■■■■■■■■■■■■■■■■■■■■■■■■■■■■■■

BIBLE STUDY GUIDE
Today's Bible Reading:
Jude 1

Sept 2

1. What type of teachers had crept into the church? v. 4 _Godless teachers who reinterpet misinterpret the Holy scriptures misguiding the flock_

2. What was their main problem? v. 8 _Dispised Gods authority_

3. What path had these false teachers taken? v. 11 _They followed the way Cain took_

TODAY'S WORLD PRAYER EMPHASIS

EUROPE - BULGARIA
- Population: 9,036,000
- Religion: Non-religious/other 17% - Muslim .13.9% - Protestant 1.25% - Roman Catholic 0.83% - Orthodox 66.9% - Marginal 0.02%
- Needs:
    Pray for Peter and Demitar, graduates of a Crossroads School of Broadcasting conducted during 1991 in Vienna. They have had some opportunity for broadcasting but need prayer that God will fully open the doors.

    Many forms of eastern and western cults, as well as the ancient occultism of Bulgaria, vie for a following. Pray that in this time of spiritual searching that the spirit of deceit will be bound and demonic forces destroyed so that these people can find their answers in Jesus Christ.

    There is severe division among the Christians in Bulgaria which leads to a diminished witness. Pray for repentance, healing, and spiritual unity so that the lost may be reached effectively.

GOD'S CIVIL AUTHORITIES

Meekness involves coming into an understanding that every human authority has been ordained and placed there by God.

This is very difficult to conceive, especially for those living under oppressive regimes. Therefore, in later lessons we will study the exceptions to the rule—situations where human authorities usurp the higher authority of God's Word and violate human dignity.

In this lesson, however, we are continuing our emphasis on what the Scripture teaches about submitting to every human authority.

Scripture requires Christians to submit to all governing authorities since they all derive their right to rule from God (Ro. 13:1-7). This includes all levels of government in the exercise of their powers to make and enforce laws, as well as to levy and collect taxes.

The person who opposes the governing authorities is opposing a divinely-appointed institution and will incur judgement (Ro. 13:2).

By obeying the civil authority, the believer is removing from unbelievers a possible source of accusation against the Church. In chapter 2, verses 13 through 15 of his First Epistle, Peter says, "Submit yourself for the Lord's sake to every authority instituted among men: whether to the king, as the supreme authority, or to governors, who are sent by him to punish those who do wrong and to commend those who do right. For it is God's will that by doing good you should silence the ignorant talk of foolish men."

The teaching of the previous section raises the question: *Should a Christian obey a government authority that is opposed to the principles of Christianity?*

Romans 13 was written to believers living under the pagan Roman government. That government would eventually become a persecutor of the Church. Yet, Christians were told to submit to their government's authority because that authority was ultimately derived from God.

This was the same Roman government that Jesus, when asked about paying taxes to Caesar, responded, "Give to Caesar what is Caesar's, and to God what is God's" (Mt. 22:21).

A Christian's duty to obey the government is not nullified just because the government might not conform to the standards of Christianity. In Scripture, Christ was very adamant that human authorities are to be obeyed.

The few times when Christians are released from their duty to obey those in leadership over them will be discussed in future lessons.

BIBLE STUDY GUIDE

Today's Bible Reading:
Matthew 22:21; Romans 13:1-6

1. What did Jesus say about obeying civil authority? Mt. 22:21 _____
_____ *Give to the emperor what is his* _____ *due and also to God his due*

2. When we rebel against authority, what do we do? Ro. 13:2 _____
_____ *If we oppose the law we oppose* _____ *God*

3. Why do we pay taxes? Ro. 13:6 _____
_____ *Pay taxes because the* _____ *authorities are working for God*

TODAY'S WORLD PRAYER EMPHASIS

ASIA - CAMBODIA
- Population: 9,205,000
- Religion: Buddhist 87% - Non-religious/other 7% - Muslim 2.9% - Animist 2.7% - Protestant 0.10% - Roman Catholic 0.28%
- Needs:
  For centuries, Cambodia has been in spiritual darkness. Ubiquitous spirit shrines, strong opposition of Buddhism to any ideological rival, and hatreds generated by 20 years of war all reveal the nature of the conflict. Pray that spirit powers which control the land may be forced to yield to the Lord Jesus.
  Pray for the young church in Cambodia. Pray specifically for freedom from government manipulation; for trained leaders to gain maturity and stop being quarrelsome and divisive; for effective Christian family witness to this nation where the family unit has been severely impaired, and the lack of morality and the use of drugs has brought about the rise in AIDS; for ministry to emotional and spiritual needs of both believers and non-believers; and vision for evangelism.

GOD'S ORDER FOR THE FAMILY

As God has placed His authority in human government, so He has placed His authority in the institution of the family.

In Ephesians, chapters 5 and 6, Paul describes for us God's perfect model for the family.

As imperfect people, we all fall short in many ways. Nevertheless, as we learn to be meek and work towards God's perfect order, our family life becomes more happy and fulfilling.

Here is God's answer for every troubled marriage and family.

God has instituted divine channels of authority within the family (Col. 3:18-21). Every disciple who would display meekness toward God must recognize and submit to these channels of authority. Our diagram illustrates this authority structure, and it also shows the spiritual equality of all the members of the family before God.

The thin line represents equality before God and the priesthood of all believers. All members of the family have direct access to the throne of God through Christ by faith (Gal. 3:28).

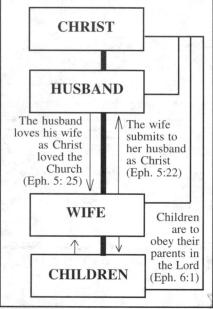

The diagram shows boxes labeled **CHRIST**, **HUSBAND**, **WIFE**, **CHILDREN**.

The husband loves his wife as Christ loved the Church (Eph. 5: 25)

The wife submits to her husband as Christ (Eph. 5:22)

Children are to obey their parents in the Lord (Eph. 6:1)

The thick line represents God's channel of governmental authority in the family. Husbands are to love their wives as Christ loved the Church and honor them (Eph. 5:25; 1 Pet. 3:1-7). The husband must submit himself in love to the needs of his wife and family in the same way that the wife is called to submit to his role as head of the family and home (Eph. 5:22-24; 1 Pet. 3:3-6).

Children are to obey and honor their parents (Eph. 6:1-3) and parents are to discipline their children with reason and love (Eph. 6:4). They must also, in a sense, learn to submit to the needs of their children, ever seeking to help them grow and mature physically, mentally, socially, and spiritually.

Anytime God's channels of governmental authority are broken, the result is disharmony within the family. This also applies to a home where the head

God Cover
Pray for Pauline
Tom
Dorothy -
Mind the many others

is an unbeliever. Though the unbeliever may not fulfill his spiritual role as a husband, that does not release the believer from submitting to God's order for authority in the home (1 Pet. 3:1-2).

■■■■■■■■■■■■■■■■■■■■■■■■■■■■■■■

BIBLE STUDY GUIDE

Today's Bible Reading:
Colossians 3:18-4:1

1. What is God's ordained rule for each member of the family? Col.3:18-21

Obedience

2. Why did Paul tell slaves to obey their masters? Col. 3:22-24

Because of ones reverence for God.

3. What was the role of a Christian slave-owner in Paul's day? Col. 4:1

to be a just a fair master because the also would stand before God on the Day of judgment

---

TODAY'S WORLD PRAYER EMPHASIS

AFRICA - CENTRAL AFRICAN REPUBLIC

- Population: 3,306,000
- Religion: Non-religious/other 1.4% - Baha'i 0.3% - Tribal religions 12.3% - Muslim 3.3% - Protestant 47.2% -Roman Catholic 34% - Marginal 1.8%
- Needs:

  Pray for the unreached peoples. There has been an influx of Muslims who present the greatest challenge at present—a task for which local believers are not yet equipped. Pray specifically for Arabs fleeing from the Sudan; the strongly Mulsim Hausa (nothing at present is being done to reach them); and the Fulani who are beginning to be reached by some of the missions groups.

  Pray for the less evangelized idigenous groups—the Pygmy Binga being evangelized by French and local missionanries; the less evangelized Sara groups along the border with Chad (some are partially Isamized); and the partly Muslim Runga in the northern tip of the country (little has been done to reach this tribe).

BEARING WITNESS AND SPEAKING OUT

Being subject to authority does not mean keeping quiet about our faith or ignoring the responsibility of speaking out against that which is in violation of God's moral law or is a social injustice. In fact, when Christians cease to be salt and light, society degenerates. The Church clearly is to be prophetic in the sense that it must raise the moral consciousness of society. In doing so, however, Christians must walk in meekness.

Christians are here on earth to proclaim the gospel and ask people to respond to God's truth. To try to forcefully establish our beliefs is clearly overstepping the boundaries of our purpose.

A great theologian once said that Christians are to *speak* the Word but not *execute* it.

Disciples of Jesus Christ must always be faithful to speak the Word by means of their verbal witness to Christ. They must also give testimony by the life they live and by their submission to the supreme authority of God's Word.

Speaking the Word is very different from *executing* the Word. Only God can woo people through the disciple's Christ-like lifestyle and verbal witness to the gospel. For example, David remained faithful to what he knew to be right, even though God anointed him as king while Saul was still ruling. Because of God's anointing, David was hunted and persecuted. Yet he would not execute his right to rule by killing Saul and taking over the kingship until God brought it to pass. Christians should be socially active in the sense of living a life of righteousness and bringing the mercy of God to people. They should proclaim God's truth against any unjust civil authority. However, they should be careful about trying to force it to conform to just principles (1 Tim. 2:1-3).

Sometimes our verbal witness will bring rejection and persecution upon us. It is then that meekness must rule our responses. We are to return love to our enemies and those who persecute us. We are to be non-retaliatory as Christ was when He was falsely accused by the authorities and abused along the road to Calvary. When Christ was asked to respond to the false accusations, rather than decrying the authorities as unfair or hypocritical, the Scripture says, "Jesus remained silent" (Mt. 26:63). He did not try to justify Himself or His actions. He agreed with those things that were true, never trying to clarify the truth. Instead, Jesus Christ went to His death asking only, "Father, forgive them, for they do not know what they are doing" (Lk. 23:34). This is the meekness to which we are called. We are to expect persecution. When it comes, we are to humble ourselves as Christ did. We are not to condemn those who persecute us; rather we are to love them.

■■

BIBLE STUDY GUIDE
Today's Bible Reading:
Acts 4:1-21, 5:17-42

1. When Peter and John appeared before the Jewish religious leaders, what were they commanded to do? Acts 4:18 _They were not to speak or teach in the Name of Jesus_

2. What was Peter's and John's response? Acts 4:19-20 _Their desire was to teach the Good News re: Christ the Only Way to God._

3. What were the accusations against the Apostles when they were arrested again? Acts 5:28 _They were accused of disobedience by High Priest & Council_

4. When ordered a second time not to preach the gospel of Christ, what did the Apostles do? Acts 5:40-42 _Once again disobeyed. They were happy to suffer for Christ's Sake_

TODAY'S WORLD PRAYER EMPHASIS

ASIA - TAIWAN
- Population: 21,507,000
- Religion: Non-religious/other 24.2% - Chinese folk religions/Buddhism 70.4% - Muslim 0.4% - Protestant 3.1% - Roman Catholic 1.6% - Marginal 0.3%
- Needs:
  The Church in Taiwan has stagnated for 30 years. Pray down the barriers to growth such as satanic bondage, resurgence in Buddhism and Taoism, divisions among Christians, the lack of pastors and full-time workers, and low commitment.
  The lack of pastors is serious. Pray for staff and students at the seminaries, and for relevant spiritual training to be provided. Pray also for more effective lay training programs that are essential to church growth and evangelism.

WHEN AUTHORITY BECOMES DESTRUCTIVE

Authority based on love for God and the highest good of the individual is God's perfect way. However, in this life, this model is only reached in various degrees. There are times when authority figures abuse those under them. This abuse can either be mental, physical, or both.

When this occurs, authorities drop below the threshold of acceptance. For example, an abused wife is in a dangerous situation. She should not stay with her husband, for in doing so she endangers her life and the lives of her children.

Neither should Christians stand by and allow social injustices to continue. Especially in democratic societies, Christians must speak out strongly against these injustices.

In his book *Celebration of Discipline*, Richard Foster makes some very perceptive comments on the limits of submission to human authority.

> The limits of the Discipline of submission are at the points at which it becomes destructive. It then becomes a denial of the law of love as taught by Jesus and is an affront to genuine biblical submission (Mt. 5, 6, 7, and especially 22:37-39).
>
> Understanding the cross-life of Jesus, Paul said, "Let every person be subject to the governing authorities" (Ro. 13:1). When Paul, however, saw that the state was failing to fulfill its God-ordained function of providing justice for all, he called it to account and insisted that the wrong be righted (Acts 16:37).
>
> Were these men in opposition to their own principle of self-denial and submission? No. They simply understood that submission reaches the end of its tether when it becomes destructive. In fact, they illustrated revolutionary subordination by meekly refusing a destructive command and being willing to suffer the consequences.

Defining limits of submission may seem easy in some cases—a person in an abusive relationship, a person ordered to violate the command of God (i.e., thou shalt not kill) by the state, and so forth. In such cases, a Christian must refuse submission, yet they should do so in a meek and humble way, completely devoid of arrogance.

The more complicated issues, however, are not so easily responded to. Because we are dealing with human relationships, some questions do not have simple answers and there is no hard and fast rule to apply to every situation.

In fact, we should be skeptical of rules which purport to cover every situation. However, the closest thing we have to a "hard and fast rule" is Peter's statement in Acts 5:29 that was mentioned earlier.

If there is a choice to be made between God and man, God's will must always be deferred to.

■■■■■■■■■■■■■■■■■■■■■■■■■■■■■■

BIBLE STUDY GUIDE

Today's Bible Reading:
Acts 16:9-40

1. What did the Roman authorities do to Paul and Silas? Acts 16:9-24

After a severe beating they were put in jail. Re: The driving out of the evil spirit

2. How did Paul call these authorities into question for their abusive behavior? Acts 16:37-40 *As wrongfully accused they demanded retraction & release —*

TODAY'S WORLD PRAYER EMPHASIS

CARIBBEAN - CUBA
- Population: 10,788,000
- Religion: Non-religious/other 30.9% - Spiritist 25% - Protestant 2.82% - Roman Catholic 41.1% - Orthodox 0.01% - Marginal 0.13%
- Needs:
  Pray that the inevitable political changes in Cuba may lead to life out of death for millions of Cubans.

  Throughout the country there is a suppressed rage. Many fear social chaos or bloody revolution in the next few years. Pray for a peaceful transition to democratic freedoms.

  Praise God for the religious resurgence that has been sweeping Cuba since the late 1980s. It is affecting every level of society. Evangelical Christians are now viewed as having a positive influence on society.

WEEKEND DEVOTIONAL GUIDE

1. *Your prayer needs:*

[handwritten notes:]
Bev & Bob - Edith Ann & Family
Marg Brum - mouth surgery
Kerry - lose of her husband Wade
Gary lose of his Mom.
Judy - " of Peter Cox.
Nan - lonely.
Louisa - Paul - conflict
Min - Illness
Bible Study -
Shauna & Wayne fam
Mike Krista
Ray & Rilla
Volunteers

• *Each week write down your newest prayer requests.*
• *After praying over them, transfer them to your main* God is Faithful Prayer List *on page 162, and remember them daily.*
• *Each time a request is answered, draw a red line through it and date it at the end.*

2. *Crossroads Christian Communications Prayer Need*

Thank the Lord for all the volunteers who help us at Crossroads. Pray that God will provide for all their needs as they give freely of their time and resources for the work of the Lord here.

3. *Lay Leadership International Prayer Need*

This week we quote Paul's request for prayer, and make it a request for the ministry of LLI. "Pray for us...that God may open a door for our message so that we may proclaim the mystery of Christ. Pray that [we] may proclaim it clearly as [we] should" (Colossians 4:3-4).

WEEKEND JOURNAL

Thoughts to reflect on and record:

1. Does my individuality, so strongly promoted in society at large, get in the way of God's desire for me to be submitted to every authority over me?

2. Are there times when I am disobedient to certain civil laws I don't like or with which I don't agree?

3. How well do I hold to God's model of love and submission in my family? Are there beliefs in my culture that I have adopted that are keeping me from fully embracing what God has said?

4. Am I verbal enough about injustices I see in society?

5. Is my view of submission balanced by the law of loving my neighbor as myself?

WHEN CONFLICTS ARISE

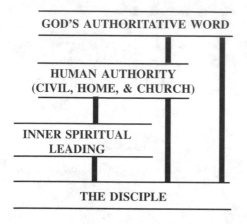

GOD'S AUTHORITATIVE WORD

HUMAN AUTHORITY
(CIVIL, HOME, & CHURCH)

INNER SPIRITUAL
LEADING

THE DISCIPLE

When conflicts arise between God's Word, human authority, and the personal leading of the Holy Spirit, what should we do?

Our diagram illustrates the supreme authority of God's Word in the life of the disciple.

If any of the human authorities God has placed in our lives require us to violate the authority of God's Word, we must ignore them and submit to His Word. We must always give precedence to the higher authority of God's Word.

When persecution arises as a result of our choice to obey the Word rather than human authority, it must be accepted in a spirit of meekness—always remembering that true meekness necessitates love rather than retaliation. The early disciples and the prophet Daniel (specifically the situation with the lions) provide examples of people who submitted to God's authority first, even though they were persecuted for it.

In matters where the will of human authority differs with what we believe is the personal leading of the Holy Spirit, we must—with patience and trust—obey the human authority...realizing that God will work circumstances for our good. However, we can and should pray that God will change the minds of those in authority over us (Acts 12:1-5).

Again, Daniel is a very good example of this approach. When he was commanded to eat the king's special food, Daniel realized that the king's desire was not to cause him to violate the law of God concerning Daniel's diet. Rather the king wanted Daniel to be healthy so that he could serve at court. In faith, Daniel proposed an alternative diet to the king. The king accepted this alternative; thus, a conflict was avoided (Dan. 1:5-16).

If these approaches—prayer and ingenuity—prove unsuccessful, we must simply pray and ask God to remove that authority over us. Yet until changes take place, we must continue to submit in areas where it does not conflict with our submission to the authority of God's Word.

God has instituted civil, familial, and church authorities in the world. True followers of Christ must recognize the God-given right of these authorities to rule. We should submit to them as part of God's will for their lives as long as these authorities do not conflict with the higher authority of God's Word.

■ ■

BIBLE STUDY GUIDE

Today's Bible Reading:
Daniel 1:3-16

1. After Daniel was turned down by the king's senior official, what did he do? Dan. 1:9-14 _Went to guard to ask why the first order, trail for 10 day Suggested change of diet_

2. What was the result of Daniel's creative and non-confrontive approach? Dan. 1:15-16 _Agreement from king guard to eat vegitables instead of what king ordered_

3. What can we learn from Daniel about personal conflicts between obeying our convictions as opposed to human authority that may arise in our own lives? _Meekness Gentleness a surrender reap its own rewards_

TODAY'S WORLD PRAYER EMPHASIS

AFRICA - DJIBOUTI
- Population: 473,000
- Religion: Muslim 94.6% - Non-religious/other 0.4% - Hindu 0.1% - Baha'i 0.1% - Protestant 0.07% - Roman Catholic 3.7% - Orthodox 1%
- Needs:
  The way opened for the first evangelical witness in 1975. Pray for the land to remain open so that strong local churches may be planted among the indigenous peoples.
  Missionary work is a tough challenge in this hot land, and working conditions are extreme. Pray for the ministries of various workers in education, public health, agriculture, literature, Bible translation, literacy, and youth work.
  Pray for the less evangelized peoples of Djibouti—the Afars, the Somalis, the Arabs, and other ethnic minorities.

CHRIST'S AUTHORITY IN HIS CHURCH

As we continue our study of what it means to be meek towards God, we need to look at another aspect of God-ordained human authority in every believer's life.

As God has willed for people to live under the authority of civil and familial government, He has also chosen for His people to be subject to human authority in the church.

In discussing leadership roles in the church, we realize that expressions and traditions in the body of Christ differ not only in how they govern themselves, but also in the terminologies used to describe different offices. However, regardless of variations in descriptions used or the type of church governments, there are usually those who fulfill three vital roles or functions:

OVERSIGHT • The twelve apostles were the first *overseers* or *elders* of the Church. Today, regardless of the tradition, in every church there are various groups of people who assume the overall leadership of Christ's church at a local, district, and national/international level. In most local churches a group of spiritually qualified people serve with a pastor to provide proper oversight over the entire church.

SERVICE MINISTRY LEADERSHIP • As the Early Church grew, the first apostles (elders) found it necessary to appoint spiritually qualified leaders to administrate the service and practical needs of the church. These first *deacons* were responsible to the apostolic leadership (Acts 6:3). Likewise, today there is a vital need for people to lead committees or local church areas of ministry and fulfill this vital administrative role. Such leadership is usually accountable to those who assume eldership and general oversight roles.

GIFTED SERVICE MINISTRY • Every believer is gifted by God and should employ whatever gifts God has given him or her in the service of others. As in the Early Church, many people who have needs today will be neglected unless ministry to them is organized (Acts 6:1-2). That's why, in most cases, local churches and Christian organizations should organize areas of ministry where believers can serve under practical and spiritually qualified leadership.

Christ desires purpose and unity in His Church. Hebrews 13:17 says, "Obey your leaders and submit to their authority. They keep watch over you as men who must give an account. Obey them so that their work will be a joy, not a burden, for that would be of no advantage to you."

Meeting the needs of a hurting world necessitates a coordinated effort. Therefore, disciples of Jesus Christ are called to submit to the leadership God has provided so that His ultimate work may be accomplished.

■■■

BIBLE STUDY GUIDE

Today's Bible Reading:
Acts 20:17-31; Hebrews 13:17

1. What is one of the most important responsibilities of church elders? Acts 20:27-30 _____

_____

_____

_____

_____

2. How are we to treat our spiritual leaders? Heb. 13:17 _____

_____

_____

_____

_____

TODAY'S WORLD PRAYER EMPHASIS

MIDDLE EAST - EGYPT
- Population: 60,470,000
- Religion: Muslim 85.4% - Non-religious/other 0.4% - Protestant 0.85% - Catholic 0.32% - Orthodox 13%
- Needs:

  David Mainse's parents spent 21 years as missionaries to Egypt and many churches were established. Pray for those churches that continue during difficult times. Crossroads' Arabic telecast, "Light For All Nations" reaches parts of Egypt. Pray that many will respond to the gospel.

  Pray that division and confusion might discredit and nullify the acts of terrorism by Islamic fundamental extremists, economic sabotage, and intolerance that is being fueled by economic stresses.

  Pray that many pastors will be raised up in this nation where nearly two-thirds of all evangelical churches have none. Pray also for those who are currently training in seminaries in Egypt, that God may strengthen them and burden them with a vision to evangelize this nation.

PASTORS AND THOSE WHO OVERSEE

The pastor (or pastors, depending upon the size of the church) is called to labor in prayer and ministry of God's Word. In most cases there is one pastor who assumes senior responsibility for those who also serve in the oversight responsibilities.

Pastors are specifically called to teach the church. In Ephesians 4:11, the teaching and pastoral gifts mentioned are synonymous. That's why in Acts chapter 6, when the first pastors became burdened down with the practical day-to-day administration of service ministry, they turned it over to others and gave themselves to their primary calling of fasting, prayer, and the ministry of God's Word.

Those who oversee or fulfill roles of eldership are to devote themselves to praying for the needs that exist among the people they are responsible for in the Lord (Acts 6:4; Phil. 1:9-11; Col. 1:9-12; Jas. 5:14-15). It is also important that elders pray to receive the mind of Christ concerning the course their church is to pursue in its Kingdom efforts.

Along with prayer, elders must also devote themselves to the study of God's Word. They must be able to accurately use the Scriptures to teach the people and rule the church according to biblical principles (2 Tim. 2:15).

Elders should also promote unity within the body of Christ. Unity among the church's leadership is the logical prerequisite to the unity of the entire body of believers which is demanded by scripture (1 Cor. 1:10; Eph. 4:1-3; Phil. 2:2). Promoting unity requires the elders to act with humility, never lording themselves over their flock. The elders should adopt an attitude of servanthood and lead in meekness according to the example of Christ (Mt. 20:25-28, 23:11-12; 2 Cor. 4:5).

This attitude of meekness and servanthood allows the elders to be patient with rebellious individuals or a body of believers who are not quite ready to obey God's directives through the elders and submit to the leadership. Although the elders should be patient, they also must be lovingly firm with those who are creating the difficulties (2 Tim. 2:24-26; Heb. 13:17).

The elders also maintain a shepherding role within the church. To do this, they must keep themselves in proper spiritual condition (Acts 20:28; 1 Tim 4:16) so as to protect the flock from false teachers (wolves). They accomplish this by being prepared to exhort in sound doctrine and refute those who contradict them (Acts 20:29-31; Titus 1:7-9).

Finally, elders are to remain free from self-interest and greed. They are to set an example in meeting the needs of others (Acts 20:33-35; 1 Pet. 5:2).

BIBLE STUDY GUIDE

Today's Bible Reading:
Acts 6:1-7; Ephesians 4:11-13

1. Why did the pastors in Jerusalem appoint the first deacons to take care of the practical needs of the church? Acts 6:2-4 _____

_____

_____

_____

_____

2. What is a pastor's chief responsibility? Eph. 4:11-12 _____

_____

_____

_____

_____

_____

_____

TODAY'S WORLD PRAYER EMPHASIS

EUROPE - SERBIA & MONTENEGRO
- Population: 10,787,394
- Religion: Non-religious/other 9% - Muslim 17% - Protestant 0.82% - Catholic 20.8% Orthodox 67% - Marginal 0.03%
- Needs:
  The Serbian Orthodox Church has a large and growing influence in both republics, but there is more nationalism than spirituality in this growth. Pray for new life in this ancient Church; there are few signs of a renewal movement.
  Montenegro is largely Orthodox by tradition and fiercely independent. There is only a small handful of Evangelicals. Pray for the calling of workers to this needy republic.

QUALIFICATIONS FOR THOSE WHO OVERSEE

As we continue our study of meekness and how it entails being subject to God's appointed human authority in His Church, let's look at the scriptural qualifications required for one who serves in an oversight role. Keep in mind that there may be some variance in structures and terminologies, but all churches have boards which assume general oversight. People who serve on these boards, according to Scripture, must fit certain qualifications. It should be noted that these qualifications in no way designate that the elder must be a full-time Christian worker or an ordained religious professional. On the contrary, in the majority of New Testament churches, it was probably qualified lay people who were appointed as elders (Acts 14:23).

In 1 Timothy 3:1-7, detailed qualifications for elders are set forth. The following is a list of those qualifications.

1.   They must desire the office (v. 1).
2.   They are to be above reproach (v. 2). This means that their conduct should be such that it could never be called into question (1 Tim. 6:13-14).
3.   They are to be the husband of one wife (v. 2). Some view this as a prohibition against polygamy while others take it to mean that an elder cannot be one who has been divorced and remarried.
4.   Elders are to be temperate (v. 2). Literally this means moderation in the use of alcoholic beverages. (See number 9 below).
5.   They are to be self-controlled (v. 2). They are prudent, thoughtful, and sensible (Titus 1:8).
6.   They are to be respectable (v. 2). This means that they are to be dignified and honorable. The term has a literal meaning of orderly.
7.   They are to be hospitable (v. 2). Literally this means one who loves strangers and opens his home to them (Ro. 12:13; Heb. 13:2).
8.   An elder is to be a good teacher (v. 2, 2 Tim. 2:24).
9.   Elders should not be drunkards (v. 3). Literally this means not addicted to wine. This qualification would cause us to interpret number (4) above metaphorically as meaning clear-headed or self-controlled (Prov. 20:1; Ro. 14:13-15:2).
10.   Elders are not to be violent (v. 3). The elder should not be one who strikes others or gets involved in brawls (Titus 1:7).
11.   Elders are to be gentle (v. 3). This means that they are to be gracious, forebearing, yielding, and kind (Titus 3:2; Jas. 3:17).
12.   Elders should not be quarrelsome (v. 3). They are to be peaceable, disinclined to fight, and not contentious (2 Tim. 2:24; Titus 3:2).
13.   They should not love money (v. 3). Elders should not be greedy, avaricious, nor covetous (Heb. 13:5).

14. Elders must manage their own household well, keeping their children submissive in every way (v. 4). Their children should respectfully live in obedience to their parents (v. 5).

15. An elder should not be a recent convert to the faith (v. 6). The danger of appointing a newly converted person to a position of authority is that they will be puffed up with pride.

16. An elder should be well thought of by outsiders (v. 7). This will preserve both the elder and the church form falling into disgrace by being caught in Satan's trap of hypocrisy.

■■■■■■■■■■■■■■■■■■■■■■■■■■■■■■■■■■■

BIBLE STUDY GUIDE

Today's Bible Reading:
1 Timothy 3:1-7

1. List some of the qualifications for elders that you feel are most important or should be stressed in today's world. _____

_____

_____

_____

_____

_____

_____

_____

_____

_____

TODAY'S WORLD PRAYER EMPHASIS

CARIBBEAN - ST. LUCIA
• Population: 164,000
• Religion: Spiritist 2% - Baha'i 1.2% - Hindu 0.9% - Muslim 0.5% - Rastafarian 0.3% - Protestant 18.2% - Roman Catholic 75.7% -Marginal 1.2%
• Needs:
  Pray for a spiritual awakening among the Christians of this nation.
  The number of churches alive in the Spirit has grown, but so have the divisions. Pray for unity among believers.
  Pray for the translation of the New Testament into French Creole (the dominant language among the islanders). Pray also that this will make the Word of God become more precious, understood, and applied to daily life.

LEADERS OF SERVICE MINISTRY

We now come to the second level of leadership in Christ's church. This is the level of leadership involved in administrating the fulfillment of the practical needs of the people.

The Early Church gave the title of *deacon* to individuals who fulfilled this role. The word *deacon* is derived form the Greek word *diakonos*, which means one who renders service. It is used in a general sense by Christ to refer to all Christian leaders (Mt. 23:10-11).

The word *deacon* is also used to refer to individuals specifically set apart in the church to carry out the directives of the elders in the practical areas of administration and service.

In the New Testament, deacons were nominated and approved by the congregation and then ordained to their ministry by prayer and the laying on of hands (Acts 6:1-6). Both men and women served in this role.

We need to keep in mind that although churches differ in their organizational structures and the titles they give these roles, these three levels of leadership usually exist in every church in some fashion or another.

Deacons provide leadership over a variety of areas. These often include caregiver outreaches, food programs, and other benevolent ministries; account and finance; ushering; building maintenance, development, and expansion; and church management and administration.

Although deacons perform a practical ministry of service, this does not prevent them from developing their spiritual gifts in other areas. They can even come to the point where they leave the office of deacon and devote all of their time to their new ministry. New Testament examples of this can be found in Stephen who became the Church's first martyr and Phillip who became an evangelist (Stephen: Acts 6:5, 8-15, 7:1-60; Phillip: Acts 6:5, 8:5-8, 8:26-40, 21:8).

Probably one of the greatest needs in today's church is to recognize the need for this second level of leadership. Unfortunately, in many churches much of these "middle-management" administrative duties have been transferred to the pastors. This burdens the pastors and greatly hampers their ministry of equipping the saints. Thus, if a church is to fulfill its role in reaching the world, there must be this second level of leadership within the local body.

■ ■

BIBLE STUDY GUIDE
Today's Bible Reading:
Acts 6:1-6

1. What was the ministry of the first deacons? Acts 6:1-3 _____
_____
_____

2. Was their ministry considered valuable spiritually? Acts 6:6 _____
_____

3. List some of the areas where you think people in need may be neglected in today's churches. Based on the example of the Early Church, what do you think should happen?_____
_____
_____
_____
_____
_____
_____

TODAY'S WORLD PRAYER EMPHASIS

AFRICA - SWAZILAND
- Population: 938,000
- Religion: Traditional religions 17.6% - Muslim 0.8% - Baha'i 0.4% - Non-religious/other 1% - Protestant 21.5% - Roman Catholic 6% - Marginal 52.5%
- Needs:
  Renewed vision for evangelism has led to church growth through many ministries. Pray for unity, growth, and holiness to characterize the Church in Swaziland. Pray also for effective ministry to the men, Mozambican refugees, and the Muslim community.
  One of the official languages of Swaziland is siSwati. Christian literature in siSwati is a vital need. The siSwati New Testament was just published in 1981. Pray for the production, distribution, and impact of the siSwati Bible when it is published in 1994.

WEEKEND DEVOTIONAL GUIDE

1. *Your prayer needs:*

• *Each week write down your newest prayer requests.*
• *After praying over them, transfer them to your main* God is Faithful
Prayer List *on page 162 and remember them daily.*
• *Each time a request is answered, draw a red line through it and date it
at the end.*

2. *Crossroads Christian Communications Prayer Need*

Pray for the "Walk of Faith," a way of honoring special people in our
lives and placing a memorial to a loved one. With God's help, we plan
to pay off the Crossroads' building debt and at the same time, surround the Crossroads Centre with God's Word. Call 1-800-668-0144
for information on how to participate.

3. *Lay Leadership International Prayer Need*

Pray for LLI's work throughout Asia, under the leadership of LLI's
World Missions Director Naomi Dowdy, as it reaches into areas of
Myanmar, China, Hong Kong, India, Indonesia, Japan, South Korea,
Malaysia, the Philippines, Singapore, and Thailand.

WEEKEND JOURNAL

Thoughts to reflect on and record:

1. When I have a conviction from the Holy Spirit and a human authority doesn't understand or agree with it, do I confront the authority and get myself in trouble, do I seek for alternatives, or do I patiently pray?

2. Do I take seriously the words of Hebrews 13:17? Do I ever make myself a burden on my spiritual overseers because I do not follow their leadership?

3. In light of the heavy spiritual responsibilities given by God to a pastor, do I, or does my church, keep my pastor busy doing things that he or she should not be doing?

4. When appointing or electing elders, how seriously do I, or does my church, consider the biblical qualifications mentioned in 1 Timothy 3:1-7?

5. Have I been aware of how important it is to have church leaders who give themselves to overseeing the practical needs and outreaches of my church?

QUALIFICATION FOR SERVICE MINISTRIES LEADERS

Even those called to leadership roles in areas of service need to be gifted in specific areas, and the Scriptures set forth a list of the spiritual qualifications needed.

According to 1 Timothy 3:8-13 and Acts 6:2-4, the following is a list of qualifications these individuals should possess.

1. They are to be worthy of respect (v. 8). This means a deacon should be serious, noble, and dignified.

2. They should be sincere (v. 8). A deacon should not be a person who says one thing to one person and then something else to another (Jas. 3:8-12).

3. They should not be given to drinking much wine (v. 8). This corresponds to number (9) for elders in the previous lesson (Prov. 23:29-35; Ro. 14:13-15:2).

4. They should not be greedy for gain (v. 8). A deacon should not be fond of dishonest gain or out to get money (1 Tim. 6:6-10).

5. Deacons should hold the mystery or deep truths of the faith with a clear conscience (v. 9). Here mystery does not refer to something unknown but that which God has now revealed by the gospel. A clear or clean conscience is one that has been cleansed by Christ's blood and knows it has done no wrong to God or humanity (Acts 24:16; Heb. 10:22).

6. Deacons should also be tested first (v. 10). The deacon's stability and Christ-like character must be approved by experience before he or she can assume responsibilities.

7. Deacons should be blameless (v. 10). Literally this means someone who cannot be called to account; i.e., someone who is irreproachable.

8. Deacons should have spouses who are "worthy of respect, not malicious talkers but temperate and trustworthy in everything" (v. 11).

9. A deacon is to be the husband of one wife (v. 12). See number (3) under elders in Lesson 29.

10. Deacons are to manage their children and their households well (v. 12). See number (14) in Lesson 29.

11. All of the above qualifications are essential because the work of a deacon is a high calling of God. "Those who have served well (as deacons) gain an excellent standing and great assurance in their faith in Christ Jesus" (v. 13).

12. They must be willing to serve tables; i.e., they must humbly take on whatever practical tasks need to be done (Acts 6:2).

13. They must be of good repute, that is, others must bear witness to their good character (v. 3).

14. They must be full of the Holy Spirit. This means that their lives should

be submitted to the Spirit's direction and empowering and they should consistently show forth the fruit of the Holy Spirit (v. 3).

15. Deacons are to be full of wisdom; i.e., they must be capable not only of discharging their administrative duties, but also of doing so with sensitivity and common sense. This is especially true when dealing with difficult and delicate situations that involve both Christians and non-Christians.

■■■■■■■■■■■■■■■■■■■■■■■■■■■■■■■■■■■

BIBLE STUDY GUIDE

Today's Bible Reading:
1 Timothy 3:8-13

List some of the spiritual qualifications for service ministry leaders that you feel are most important and should be stressed in today's world._____

_____

_____

_____

_____

_____

_____

_____

_____

TODAY'S WORLD PRAYER EMPHASIS

EUROPE - SWITZERLAND
- Population: 6,552,000
- Religion: Non-religious/other 7.7% - Muslim 1% - Jewish 0.3% - Protestant 42% - Roman Catholic 47.2% - Other Catholic 0.3% - Orthodox 1.1% - Marginal 1.4%
- Needs:
  Crossroads has had graduates of the television course working in Switzerland for 8 years now. Pray for greater opportunity to share the gospel.
  Membership in the church has declined over the last 30 years as wealth, comfort, indifference, and vague religiosity have become the norm. Pray that the Swiss may find the true way in Jesus Christ, and that the nation might again witness the outpouring of the Holy Spirit.

EVERYONE IS GIFTED TO SERVE

OVERSIGHT
ROLES

SERVICE MINISTRY
LEADERSHIP ROLES

GIFTED SERVICE
MINISTRY ROLES

The final level, or role, in Christ's church includes everyone.

God has gifted each person to serve others in some specific area. Therefore, meekness also includes submitting to our individual roles as service members of His church.

All believers are called to influence society by means of their lifestyle. We are constantly to demonstrate the principles of God's kingdom at work in our lives and in our contacts with others (Mt. 5:13). In doing this, we bear witness of the gospel by means of our good works as well as our words of testimony of Christ in our community and our places of work (Mt. 5:14-16).

Also, as believers we are commanded by Scripture to submit to those who have positions of leadership and to imitate their godly lifestyle. We are to appreciate them and edify them by meekly submitting to their leadership (Heb. 13:7, 17; 1 Thes. 5:12-13).

As we submit to and learn from the leadership in our church, we must commit ourselves to the path of discipleship. We must study and grow in our knowledge and experience the principles of God's kingdom.

In this way, we will become mature and stable disciples, discovering and developing our spiritual gifts and putting them to use by being involved in an area of service to others (Ro. 12:6-8; 1 Pet. 4:10-11).

Finally, regardless of position, all believers are expected to contribute to the support of the work of God. This would include all the undertakings to which the church is committed; e.g., salaries, building funds, missions, supporting other local ministries, and so forth (1 Tim. 5:17-18).

Unfortunately, in many churches the number of outreaches are limited because of lack of involvement by believers. There is a great need for believers to begin to use the gifts God has given them for His service.

There is also a need for more cooperation within the entire body of Christ and the pooling of resources that are necessary for ministering to the complex needs of hurting people in the world today.

BIBLE STUDY GUIDE

Today's Bible Reading:
Mt. 5:14-16; 1 Thes. 5:12-13; 1 Pet. 4:10-12

1. What should the end result be for those who are growing in Christ's character? Mt. 5:14-16 _____

_____

_____

_____

_____

2. Why is it important to discover and use whatever spiritual gifts God has given you? 1 Pet. 4:10-12 _____

_____

_____

_____

3. How should we regard those who lead us in the church? 1 Thes. 5:12-13

_____

_____

_____

_____

_____

TODAY'S WORLD PRAYER EMPHASIS

CARIBBEAN - TRINIDAD & TOBAGO
- Population: 1,451,000
- Religion: Non-religious/other 9.1% - Hindu 24.3% - Muslim 5.9% - Baha'i 0.9% - Protestant 28% - Roman Catholic 29.9% - Orthodox 0.5% - Marginal 1.4%
- Needs:
  The Prime Minister of this nation is a Christian. Pray for the government and religious leaders as they seek to bring harmony to Trinidad & Tobago.
  A cross-cultural vision is lacking in most churches. Pray for a greater awareness of local and world needs, and for effective training to be given in cross-cultural outreach.
  Pray for the Christian media ministries. Pray for the workers as well as the radio and television programs that they might work together to reach this nation.

FOLLOWING THE SPIRIT'S LEADING

Now we enter the third area of what it means to be meek and submitted to God's authority. This area is the realm of obeying the inner leading of God's Holy Spirit.

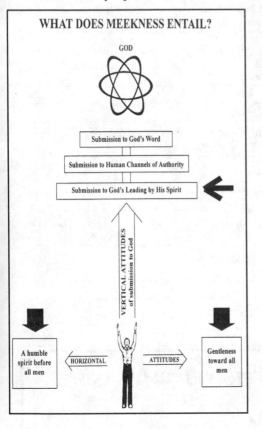

WHAT DOES MEEKNESS ENTAIL?

GOD

Submission to God's Word

Submission to Human Channels of Authority

Submission to God's Leading by His Spirit

VERTICAL ATTITUDES of submission to God

A humble spirit before all men

HORIZONTAL   ATTITUDES

Gentleness toward all men

When Christ spoke about the coming of the Holy Spirit, He declared that the Spirit would be our Counselor (Jn.14:16, 16:17). The Holy Spirit is the One who is always at our side to give us guidance for our lives.

Early in His life, Christ, our great example, was led by the Spirit into the wilderness. Likewise, the Scriptures teach that the Holy Spirit is involved in leading Christians today.

In Romans 8:14, we are told that those who are God's children are led by the Spirit of God. This is a strong statement—one which indicates that true believers can be discerned by how they accept the Holy Spirit's leading in their lives.

The inner voice, or leading of God's Spirit is a very real and definite experience that every believer can enjoy. Yet there needs to be much care and wisdom in order for one to be assured that what they believe they sense and feel is really a leading from God.

If a Christian does not understand the principles of guidance surrounding the leading of the Spirit, he or she can be led astray by imagination and even be led into error. The sincere follower of Christ needs to confirm the Spirit's leading, and when he or she is sure of His direction, obey what He is saying.

For example, in the Early Church Paul and his companions were told by the Holy Spirit not to go into Asia but rather to go to Macedonia and they followed His leading; Peter was led by the Holy Spirit to preach to the house of Cornelius; and Paul was instructed by the Spirit to go to Jerusalem even though he was warned that it would mean persecution and imprisonment. In each case, once the men were sure of the Spirit's leading, they followed it, facing whatever they encountered with meekness and humility.

The Holy Spirit does lead and demand obedience, but He also confirms His leading in many different ways. In the lessons ahead, we will look at how we can know that the Holy Spirit is truly guiding us.

■■■■■■■■■■■■■■■■■■■■■■■■■■■■

BIBLE STUDY GUIDE
Today's Bible Reading:
John 14:16-18, 26; 15: 7-16; Romans 8:14

1. What name did Jesus give the Holy Spirit in John 14:16? Based on this name, what things can we look to the Holy Spirit for? _____

_____

2. What should a child of God expect? Ro. 8:14 _____

_____

_____

3. Describe ways in which you have experienced the leading of the Holy Spirit. _____

_____

_____

_____

TODAY'S WORLD PRAYER EMPHASIS

AFRICA - TANZANIA
• Population: 32,892,000
• Religion: Muslim 35% - Traditional religions 13.2% - Baha'i 0.4% - Hindu 0.1%
    Protestant 19% - Roman Catholic 31.2% - Orthodox 0.04% - Marginal 0.77%
• Needs:
    Pray that the pressures to increase Islamic influence across the country may fail and that Christians may exert a wholesome influence at every level of society.
    Pray for church teaching programs aimed at slowing the spread of AIDS and for counselling clinics and care structures for victims.
    Pray for the less reached—the people of Zanzabar and Pemba; the Muslim coastal peoples; the peoples on the Mozambique borders; those still trapped in traditional religions that preach about demons and witchcraft; and for people in urban areas whom the church is not yet equipped to reach.

THE VOICE OF THE SPIRIT IN PRAYER

The leading of God's Holy Spirit occurs as we consistently spend time with Him in prayer. Whether it's in our daily quiet time or as we go about our work, the voice of the Holy Spirit can and will be heard if we turn our thoughts to Him and wait patiently upon Him.

The foundation for being led by the Holy Spirit is prayer. Prayer sets the stage for hearing God's voice. One only has to look at the example of Jesus to see the importance of solitude in prayer.

Luke points out to us that Christ prayed frequently, "But Jesus often withdrew to lonely places and prayed" (5:16). Through Mark we learn that Christ prayed privately in a place free from distraction or interruptions, "Very early in the morning, while it was still dark, Jesus got up, left the house and went off to a solitary place, where he prayed" (1:35).

In Matthew 6:5-14, Jesus himself taught us how to pray. First, He said we were to find a private place. Then He told us not to pray with empty repetitiveness as the heathen do. It is not the number of words spoken that constitutes effective prayer, rather it's how we pray.

Finally, Jesus gave us a model for prayer—a perfect plan to follow in our daily worship and devotional prayer time. In the Lord's Prayer, we are told to begin by worshiping God the Father and reflecting on who He is. Then we pray for His kingdom and will to be accomplished in the lives of our family, friends, church, government, as well as in us.

This is followed by prayer for personal needs as we ask for our daily bread. We continue by seeking personal cleansing and forgiving others who have wronged us. We proceed to seek His protection from temptation and the evil one. We then can end our prayer time by once again praising Him for who He is—the Lord and ruler over all kingdoms forever.

As we learn to seek God as Christ instructed, we open ourselves to the inner voice of the Holy Spirit. Prayer can also spill over into our daily lives as we learn to practice the presence of Jesus Christ throughout our day's activities. As we drive or walk, as we wait for an appointment, or in numerous other daily situations, our hearts can be in communication with Him—worshiping Him for who He is, praying for the needs of others, bringing personal needs before Him, seeking His will, forgiving others, and seeking His protection from temptations. Throughout the day we can be in His presence—hearing His voice and obeying the leading of His Holy Spirit.

Meek people are those who seek to be submissive to the voice of the Holy Spirit through prayer.

BIBLE STUDY GUIDE

Today's Bible Reading:
Mt. 6:6-14; Mk. 1:35; Lk. 5:16

1. Where and how we pray is important. Where did Jesus tell us to pray and how did He do this in His own personal life? Mt. 6:6; Lk. 5:16; Mk. 1:35

_____

_____

_____

_____

2. Jesus gave us an outline to follow in our prayer times. This can be done in 5 minutes or 5 hours. Try praying as He instructed in Matthew 6:9-13.

> *Our Father* - Spend time praising Him for His love and for who He is.
>
> *Hallowed be your name* - Reflect on His holiness.
>
> *Thy kingdom come, Thy will be done* - Pray for God's will in the lives of family, friends, and neighbors, government leaders, etc.
>
> *Give us this day* - Present your personal needs.
>
> *Forgive us our debts* - Confess your known and unknown sins.
>
> *Lead us not into temptation* - Pray for the Lord to protect and keep you from the enemy.

TODAY'S WORLD PRAYER EMPHASIS

CARIBBEAN - TURKS & CAICOS ISLANDS
- Population: 10,730
- Religion: Non-religious/other 1% - Protestant 84.5% - Roman Catholic 12% - Marginal 2.5%
- Needs:
  Corruption and drug scandals have rocked the church-going islanders. Pray that Christian values may permeate every level of society.
  Non-Christian (i.e., Marginal) religions are growing 10 times faster than Christianity. Pray that God will move in this nation and more and more people will turn to His salvation.

PROCEED WITH CAUTION

In seeking the leading of God's Holy Spirit, we must know how to test and confirm what we believe He is saying.

Hannah Whitall Smith, in her classic *The Christians Secret of a Happy Life*, says the following:

> We must never forget that 'impressions' can come from other sources as well as from the Holy Spirit. The strong personalities of those around us are the source of a great many of our impressions. Impressions also arise often from our wrong physical conditions, which color things far more than we dream. And finally, impressions come from those spiritual enemies which seem to lie in wait for every traveler who seeks to enter the higher regions of the spiritual life. In the same epistle which tells us that we are seated in 'heavenly places in Christ' (Eph. 2:6), we are also told that we shall have to fight there with spiritual enemies (Eph. 6:12). These spiritual enemies, whoever or whatever they may be, must necessarily communicate with us by means of our spiritual faculties; and their voices therefore will be, as the voice of God is, an inward impression made upon our spirits. Consequently, just as the Holy Spirit may tell us by impressions what is the will of God concerning us, so also will these spiritual enemies tell us by impression what is their will concerning us—disguising themselves, of course, as 'angels of light' who have come to lead us closer to God.
>
> Many earnest and honest-hearted children of God have been thus deluded into paths of extreme fanaticism, all the while thinking they were closely following the Lord. God, who sees the sincerity of their hearts, can and does, I am sure, pity and forgive; but the consequences as to this life are often very sad. It is not enough to have a 'leading'; we must find out the source of that leading before we give ourselves up to follow it. It is not enough either, for the leading to be very 'remarkable,' or the coincidences to be very striking, to stamp it as being surely from God. In all ages of the world, evil and deceiving agencies have been able to work miracles, foretell events, reveal secrets, and give 'signs'; and God's people have always been emphatically warned about being deceived thereby.

We test the Spirit's leading in four primary ways: (1) through the confirmation of Scripture; (2) through godly confidants; (3) through mutual cooperation when it involves other people; and (4) by testing the circumstances.

When these areas have been checked and there is peace about a situation, then one can move forward and, in faith, take action in the direction the Holy Spirit is leading.

BIBLE STUDY GUIDE

Today's Bible Reading:
Ex. 7:8-12; 1 Cor. 11:13-15; 1 Jn. 4:1

1. How does Satan often try to deceive us? 1 Cor. 11:13-15 _____

_____

_____

_____

_____

2. What were people who were given over to the occult able to do in front of Aaron and Moses? Ex. 7:8-12 _____

_____

_____

_____

3. What does John tell us to do in 1 John 4:1? _____

_____

_____

_____

_____

TODAY'S WORLD PRAYER EMPHASIS

AFRICA - UGANDA
- Population: 22,012,000
- Religion: Muslim 8% - Traditional religions 5.9% - Baha'i 2.7% - Protestant 30% - Roman Catholic 52% - Orthodox 0.14% - Marginal 1.21%
- Needs:
    Currently Uganda has the highest known incidence of AIDS in the world. Due to a spectacular moral collapse over the last 20 years, an estimated 25-30% of the people of this nation had the virus in 1992 and the number steadily climbs. Pray for a move of God in this nation that can bring the people out of this terrible cycle of immorality and disease.
    Pray for the Church as it faces up to the tribalism that has plagued it for years. Much of the anarchy within the nation in recent years is a reuslt of inner-ethnic hatreds which has also infected the Church.

WEEKEND DEVOTIONAL GUIDE

1. *Your prayer needs:*

• *Each week write down your newest prayer requests.*
• *After praying over them, transfer them to your main* God is Faithful
Prayer List *on page 162 and remember them daily.*
• *Each time a request is answered, draw a red line through it and date it
at the end.*

2. *Crossroads Christian Communications Prayer Need*

Pray for a renewed vision in all our hearts to boldly go forth with the
gospel across our nation. Pray that David Mainse's vision will remain
strong and focused as he listens to God's voice and follows His leading.

3. *Lay Leadership International Prayer Need*

Pray for LLI's financial needs. Pray that God will open every door
and supply every need as *Life by Design* is launched on TV stations in
the United States.

WEEKEND JOURNAL

Thoughts to reflect on and record:

1. Am I ready and willing to lead or be led in meeting the practical needs of people either through a Christian organization or my local church?

2. Am I ready and willing to go beyond the church walls and share God's love in practical ways through involvement in my community?

3. Am I sensitive to the inner voice of the Holy Spirit? Do I submit my plans and ways to Him daily?

4. Am I taking time not only to pray, but to listen to what God is trying to say to me each day?

5. Do I seek to confirm the leading of the Holy Spirit through the Word, godly confidants, mutual cooperation, and the testing of circumstances?

FOLLOWING THE PRINCIPLES OF SCRIPTURE

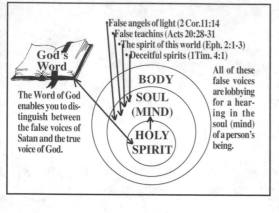

False angels of light (2 Cor.11:14
False teachins (Acts 20:28-31
The spirit of this world (Eph. 2:1-3)
Deceitful spirits (1Tim. 4:1)

God's Word

The Word of God enables you to distinguish between the false voices of Satan and the true voice of God.

BODY
SOUL (MIND)
HOLY SPIRIT

All of these false voices are lobbying for a hearing in the soul (mind) of a person's being.

The Holy Spirit living within us gives us spiritual eyes to distinguish what voices are from God and what voices are from some other source. He does this by illuminating the truth of God's Word to our minds so that every opinion and philosophy can be measured against it.

The Word of God is the ultimate vehicle God uses to speak to His children. It is the supreme factor upon which we judge all other opinions and philosophies.

Because we live in a fallen and imperfect world (as our diagram shows), there are many voices lobbying for a hearing in our minds. The Bible speaks of false prophets who may twist the Scripture or subtly change its meaning so that the unobservant will think they really are being taught the Word of God. Closely akin to these misguided individuals are false teachers who use the Word of God cunningly. There are also the philosophies or counsels of this world and its deceitful spirits who seek to deceive us into believing that something is from God when it is not.

Although our minds perceive many possible sources of direction, as we study the principles of the Scriptures we can sort out those which are of God and those which are not. The principles of the Scriptures enable us to separate out those voices which are not of God, and speak only to our mind.

Our communication with God in the realm of the Spirit must always be within the confines of the principles of God's Word. Only a constant awareness of the principles of the Word will protect us from erring in our judgment as to what is and what is not God's voice.

Joshua serves as an example in this area. When God chose him to lead Israel into the possession of the Promised Land, He told Joshua: "Be strong and very courageous. Be careful to obey all the law my servant Moses gave you; do not turn from it to the right or the left, that you my be successful wherever you go. Do not let this Book of the Law depart from your mouth; meditate on it day and night, so that you may be careful to do everything written in it. Then you will be prosperous and successful" (Josh. 1:7-8).

Only the Word of God would keep Joshua from being distracted in his calling and conquest. Close adherence would determine his success and prosperity.

Like Joshua, we must meditate day and night upon biblical truths so that we know beyond a shadow of a doubt what is true and can therefore identify what is false (2 Tim. 3:14-15). When we think God wants us to move in a certain direction, we must ask Him to confirm it in His Word.

■■■■■■■■■■■■■■■■□■■■■■■■■■■■■■■■■■■■■■■■■

BIBLE STUDY GUIDE
Today's Bible Reading:
Jos. 1:8; Psa. 1; Acts 17:10-15; Eph. 4:14

1. What did the Bereans do that should serve as an example for every Christian? Acts 17:11_____

_____

2. What happens to people who ground themselves in God's Word? Eph. 4:14; Psa. 1:2-3 ____ _____

_____

3. What did God say would guarantee Joshua's success? Jos. 1:8 _____

_____

TODAY'S WORLD PRAYER EMPHASIS

MIDDLE EAST - UNITED ARAB EMIRATES
- Population: 2,176,000
- Religion: Hindu 4.7% - Muslim 84.6% - Buddhist 1% - Non-religious/other 1% - Protestant 1% - Roman Catholic 4.5% - Orthodox 3.2%
- Needs:
  The radical changes of the last 20 years have helped put UAE citizens in daily contact with foreign Christians. However, these Christians are not always open to sharing their faith because of increasing political restrictions. Pray for courage, wisdom, and open hearts in this nation.

  Pray for the many expatriate congregations within the UAE, that they may strengthen their faith and evangelize the country.

  Pray for the unreached peoples—the indigenous Arab population and many expatriate communities such as the migrant Irani (Persian, Kurd, Baloch), Pakistani (Punjabi, Pushtun, Baloch), Somalis, Sudanese, and Thai which have no known groups of believers among them.

TALKING WITH FRIENDS AND CONFIDANTS

The second way we test or confirm the Holy Spirit's leading is through consulting with other godly confidants. Though no person can tell you what God's will is for you personally, true friends can help you understand more clearly what it is you may be hearing from God.

Jesus said, "Where two or three come together in my name, there I am with them" (Mt. 18:20). In the unity of fellowship and prayer together we can expect the Lord to impress upon our hearts and minds His will for us. This is why every Christian should be part of a small circle of Christians who meet regularly for prayer and who are able to share honestly and assist each other in determining God's will.

However, there are some cautions that should be observed in this area. For example, not everyone is confidential and mature enough to handle some of the things you might want to share. A person needs to be careful that those who listen are capable of constructive support, love, and confidentiality.

Observing the levels of relationships in Jesus' life is very helpful in determining who to share your questions with. First, He related to the multitudes. He loved them, ministered to them, and met their needs. However, He did not share His deepest thoughts with them. Believers need to be careful about what they share with a crowd. It is often misinterpreted and a wrong image construed.

Second, Jesus maintained a relationship with the 70. These were the people who followed Him, heard His public teaching, and were called disciples. There is no record that Christ ever shared beyond a task-oriented level with the 70. For the disciple today, just because you know and work closely with someone does not mean that person is one you should look to for help in certain levels of guidance.

Third, Jesus reserved showing His heart for the Twelve. To them He was open with His vision and His feelings. That's why the small group concept is so important in our personal Christian growth today.

Fourth, Christ had a relationship with three of the Twelve—Peter, James, and John—that He did not have with the others. He allowed them to witness His transfiguration and told them not to reveal what they saw to the others. This shows that there is a deeper level of trust that can be built in a believer's life. It is here one can share confidentially what they believe God is saying to them. They can do it without fear of reprisal if it proves to be wrong.

Fifth, Christ shared with John more than all the rest. There are private areas of life where sensitive information relative to God's personal leading needs to be discussed either with a close friend, a pastor, or possibly a counselor. Make sure, such persons are listeners of unconditional acceptance, and wisdom.

The witness and wisdom of godly confidants can greatly assist us in ascertaining God's leading and will, but they cannot tell us God's will for our lives. However, the Holy Spirit can and often will use them to give us new insights into how God may be leading us.

■■■■■■■■■■■■■■■■■■■■■■■■■■■■■■■■■■■

BIBLE STUDY GUIDE

Today's Bible Reading:
Matthew 17:1-9, 18:18-20

1. What is the Lord's promise when we share with one or two others?
Mt. 18:18-20 _____

_____

_____

2. Did Jesus include all twelve of His disciples in everything He shared?
Mt. 17:1-9 _____

_____

_____

TODAY'S WORLD PRAYER EMPHASIS

NORTH AMERICA - UNITED STATES OF AMERICA
- Population: 258,204,000
- Religion: Non-religious/other 8.7% - Jewish 2.4% - Muslim 1.8% - Hindu 0.2% - Baha'i 0.02% - Buddhist 0.4% - Protestant 51.3% - Roman Catholic 28% - Other Catholic 0.2% - Orthodox 3% - Marginal 4%
- Needs:
  Pray for Crossroads USA and for the Crossroads television productions in the U.S., including *100 Huntley Street*; *Circle Square*, and *Kingdom Adventure* for Children; *Inside Track* for teens; and *Talk to Me*, hosted five nights a week by Jim Cantelon, covering all 50 states.

  There are signs of a spiritual awakening in the U.S. Pray that God will pour out His Spirit upon this nation, allowing the awakening to be strengthened into a full-fledged revival.

  Pray for ministries that reach out to the increasingly violent inner-cities. Pray for the saftey of the laborers as well as a fruitful harvest.

THE VALUE OF COOPERATION

The third way to confirm and test the leading of the Spirit lends itself more to when such leading involves others. Sometimes it affects a spouse and family, or it may affect a local church body or area of ministry. In such cases, God guides by means of cooperation and unity that is achieved among people as they counsel together in seeking His will. This principle must be carefully adhered to, particularly with reference to finding and fulfilling our God-given ministry. If we have a particular ministry to fulfill, it is important not to move ahead until we have the approval and support of our local church or Christian organization in which we can serve. This is essential because so often it requires unity of purpose and cooperation among many believers in order to accomplish His will (Phil. 2:1-2).

What is true in the church also can be applied in the home. One person should never arbitrarily make a decision at the expense of a partner—both should feel right about the step being taken. In working with other people, even as a leader, this is a valuable principle to understand. Your vision and leading may be from God, but it will take the cooperation of others before it can be carried out.

Such was the case of leadership in Israel. Joshua and Caleb were the two spies who, along with Moses, knew it was God's will to go into Caanan. The people, however, refused to move. Did Joshua and Caleb leave the camp saying, "We will do it ourselves"? No, they waited 40 years until a new generation arose who were willing to accomplish the vision and purpose of God for the people (Nu. chs. 13-14).

In today's highly individualistic society, there are numerous role models who try to instruct us to move on our own. Leadership is seen in the string of individuals who stand against the crowd and do it their way regardless of the feelings of others. Because of the emphasis on individualism, many Christians fail to see the importance God places on unity among His people.

Psalm 133 beautifully portrays God's wonderful blessing upon people who dwell together in unity. Throughout the Word of God, the key to spiritual unity and success is cooperation in a common effort—pulling together in love to accomplish the purpose.

For those who lead, it is important to articulate and stick to a vision God gives. The Holy Spirit, however, is as patient with others as He is with you. Even though it may be very difficult at times, it may take only the Holy Spirit's fruit of patience for circumstances and time to change or bring strong wills around to what you know the Lord really desires.

BIBLE STUDY GUIDE

Today's Bible Reading:
Nu. 13:26-32, 14:26-30; Jos. 1:1-15; Psa. 133

1. Even though Joshua and Caleb disagreed profusely with their fellow spies and the rebellion of Israel, did they choose to break away and conquer the land themseleves? Nu. 13:26-32, 14:26-30; Jos. 1:1-5. What should this say to us about the value of patience until there is unity in the body of Christ? _____

_____

_____

_____

_____

2. What happens when people choose to be unified in their endeavors? Psa. 133:1-3 _____

_____

_____

_____

TODAY'S WORLD PRAYER EMPHASIS

EURASIA - UZBEKISTAN
  • Population: 23,377,000
  • Religion: Muslim 68.2% - Non-religious/other 26.1% - Jews 0.46% - Buddhist 0.3%
    Baha'i 0.2% - Protestant 0.13% - Roman Catholic 0.2% - Marginal 13.8% -
    Orthodox 4.4%
  • Needs:
    Pray for the unreached peoples—the Uzbeks (especially for the Ferghana Valley, where Islam is being revived); the Karakalpak; and the Persians (no Christians are known to be among them).
    Pray for the leaders of the nation who are faced with the daunting task of rebuilding Uzbekistan politically, economically, socially, and ecologically. There is already tension between democratic reformers and Islamic fundamentalists. Pray for wisdom for those in power.

THE ROLE OF CIRCUMSTANCES

The fourth area that helps us confirm and test the inner leading of God's Holy Spirit is circumstances.

For example, both Moses and Joshua sent spies into the Promised Land. Was this a lack of faith? Certainly not. They wanted to know if it was God's time for the people to cross the Jordan. They were looking for some positive signs that said "now is the time to move."

Sometimes we may feel an impression from God to move in a certain direction. We should, however, make sure the doors are opening and see God's ordering of circumstances before we step out presumptuously.

An example of such presumption can be found in a godly man and his wife who were deeply committed Christians and felt the call to go to South America as missionaries.

In faith, this godly couple sold their home and furniture and made preparations to go where God had called them. Circumstances, however, were not right. In fact, they did not leave for South America for 8 years following the sale of their home. Rather than be certain that the time for them to go was immediate, they had moved ahead presumptuously and ignored God's perfect timing. They had heard His call correctly, but they failed to check the circumstances to see if it was time to move.

While circumstances can help us to determine God's timing, we must not allow ourselves to be totally ruled by them.

Just because circumstances are not favorable does not mean we should change our minds about what we know is God's will.

God has promised that His wisdom will guide us as we await His perfect time (Jas. 1:5-8).

Circumstances which with may be blocking the way to fulfilling God's will can be changed through prayer (Mt. 17:20-21).

Like Paul, we must remain sensitive to God's intervention in our circumstances in order to show us His timing and perfect will (Acts 16:6-10).

It is important that we do not use circumstances as the primary means of determining God's leading. Rather, circumstances should be used as an indicator of *when* we should step out in faith and follow the leading of His Spirit that has been determined through other means.

BIBLE STUDY GUIDE

Today's Bible Reading:
Acts 16:6-10; James 1:2-8

1. When things don't seem to be going smoothly, what does James say we need to do? Jas. 1:2-5 _____

_____

2. If we are convinced about where God is leading us and things are still not going well, what are we to do? Jas. 1:6-8 _____

_____

_____

3. What do closed doors sometimes say to us? Acts 16:6-10 _____

_____

_____

_____

TODAY'S WORLD PRAYER EMPHASIS

LATIN AMERICA - VENEZUELA
- Population: 22,213,000
- Religion: Spiritist/animist 2.4% - Non-religious/other 2.3% - Muslim 0.42% - Baha'i 0.2% - Buddhist 0.12% - Jewish 0.1% - Protestant 5.34% - Roman Catholic 87.7% - Other Catholic 0.02% - Orthodox 0.15% - Marginal 1.36%
- Needs:

  Pray for the leadership of this nation. With drug-trafficking and corruption rampant, pray that God will raise up leadership that honors Him and values justice and fairness.

  Praise God for a spiritual breakthrough in Venezuela! However, the country is still steeped in spiritism and there has been a rapid growth in New Age and eastern cults. Pray that God will strengthen His Church in this nation. Pray also for unity within the church and and strong moral witness to a society facing rapid moral decline.

STEPPING OUT IN FAITH

There comes a time when God imparts an inner confirmation of faith to the seeking individual. Matthew 17:20—faith that moves mountains—and Hebrews 11:1—being certain of what we hope for and cannot see—becomes a reality. There is a confident, God-given assurance that what God has been saying is now going to happen.

James 2:17-26 makes it very clear that genuine faith is only completed by action. For example, Moses and Joshua led the children of Israel through the wilderness and into the Promised Land on faith (Ex. 14:15, 21; Josh. 3:14-16).

However, because we are human, we sometimes run into things that hinder our acting in faith. For example, some people are like Moses. They feel that they are unable to accomplish anything worthwhile. Even when God clearly shows them what He wants them to do, they refuse to act, saying that they do not have the necessary abilities (Ex. 4:10-13). However, 1 Corinthians 1:26-27 points out that God does not call many people who are particularly talented.

The Apostles are a good illustration of this fact. There was nothing out of the ordinary about those 12 men. Jesus called them, not on the bases of what they were, but on the basis of what He knew He could make them.

In 2 Corinthians 12:9, God tells Paul, "My power shows up best in weak people" (TLB). God leads us not on the basis of what we are, but of what He can accomplish through us as we place ourselves in His hands and act in faith. He does not require us to have unusual abilities, only an ability to trust Him to accomplish great things through us.

Just as some suffer from feelings of inadequacies, other people suffer from indecision or an inability to make a decision and see it through with God's help.

Once we have prayed for wisdom, ascertained God's will, and received His faith to carry out that will, we must move ahead in faith if God is going to be able to work through us (Jas. 1:6-8).

Finally, some people fall victim to procrastination. This is not quite the same as indecision. The indecisive person is never sure of what he or she should do next. The procrastinator knows what should be done, but holds back—usually because of some underlying fear. Sometimes the need for more prayer is used as an excuse to cover up our procrastination. As the Living Bible puts it, God had to tell Moses at the Red Sea: "Quit praying and get the people moving! Forward, March!" (Ex. 14:15).

Once we have determined the Spirit's leading—with the help of prayer, the principles of the Word, the counsel of other believers, and the testing of circumstances—and we find the doors are open, *it is then time for action...time to step out in faith*!

■■■■■■■■■■■■■■■■■■■■■■■■■■■■■■■

BIBLE STUDY GUIDE

Today's Bible Reading:
Deut. 1:1-45; Mt. 13:53-58, 17:14-23; Mk. 6:5-6; Heb. 3:7-10

1. Why did Israel not enter into the promised land? Deut. 1:32-35; Heb. 3:7-10 _____

_____

_____

_____

_____

_____

2. Study the following scriptures that show how we can hinder God's leading and work on our behalf.

    a. Matthew 13:58

    b. Matthew 17: 19-21

    c. Mark 6:5-6

TODAY'S WORLD PRAYER EMPHASIS

CARIBBEAN - VIRGIN ISLANDS
• Population: 121,000
• Religion: Non-religious/other 1.5% - Spiritist/Rastafarian 0.5% - Baha'i 0.5% - Jewish 0.5% - Protestant 58.7% - Roman Catholic 34.4% - Orthodox 0.6% - Marginal 3.5%
• Needs:
    Praise God there has been growth in His Church through witness! Pray that in this crucial time His body of believers will seek unity and a shared vision for evangelism.
    Even with the recent growth in the Church, there are still many islanders who do not know the saving grace of Jesus Christ. Pray for revival in this nation.
    Tourism has wreaked havoc on the social and moral fiber of the islands.
    Pray for evangelization of tourists, as well as those involved in the crime "industry"—drug trafficking, prostitution, and so forth.

WEEKEND DEVOTIONAL GUIDE

1. *Your prayer needs:*

• *Each week write down your newest prayer requests.*
• *After praying over them, transfer them to your main* God is Faithful
Prayer List *on page 162 and remember them daily.*
• *Each time a request is answered, draw a red line through it and date it*
at the end.

2. *Crossroads Christian CommunicationsPrayer Need*

Pray for Don Hill as he does his commentaries on *100 Huntley Street*.
Pray that he will be inspired daily to share the truths of God's Word.

3. *Lay Leadership International Prayer Need*

Pray for Sue Montgomery, our cheif editor on the *Life by Design* project.
Pray that there will be an unusual flow and direction of the Holy Spirit
upon Sue and others who work with her in preparing the final scripts
and manuscripts for the series.

WEEKEND JOURNAL

Thoughts to reflect on and record:

1. Am I consulting God to confirm His leading through the Scriptures?

2. Do I have a small group of godly confidants with whom I feel I can openly share my vision, hurts, and other concerns in an atmosphere of unconditional acceptance and love?

3. Am I willing to be patient with others in the body of Christ who are slower to catch the vision God has given ?

4. When I think I know God's will and yet things aren't working out, do I seek the Lord's wisdom on the matter? Am I open to a change in plans or, after seeking God, if that doesn't seem to be what He is saying, am I ready to hang in there regardless of what comes my way until He changes circumstances for His glory?

5. Have there been times when I know I have been disobedient to God because of unbelief? Am I willing to work at not allowing my fears to hold me back from God's best?

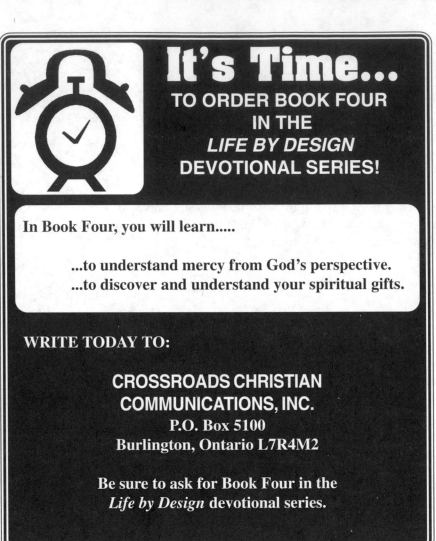

Section III:

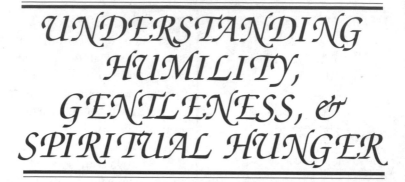

UNDERSTANDING HUMILITY, GENTLENESS, & SPIRITUAL HUNGER

> There are two other aspects of meekness that prove more difficult to understand than submission to authority. First is the call of Christ to be humble—sacrificially serving others regardless of our own rank or position in society. Because most come to Christ wanting to be served, some never discover that the greatest blessing is really found in serving others.
>
> Beyond servanthood, Christ also calls us to gentleness. To love everyone—even our enemies—often seems too difficult to handle. Yet our Lord desires to teach us how to love others, just as He loves us.

"Blessed are those who hunger and thirst for righteousness, for they will be filled" (Matthew 5:6)

> Not much is ever accomplished without passion. Spiritual hunger is that burning desire that motivates disciples to persevere until they are fully satisfied with the joys of knowing Christ.
>
> For those who lack such passion, there is great hope. The secret of developing it can be yours as you take certain steps in your ongoing walk with the Lord.

MEEKNESS MEANS HUMILITY

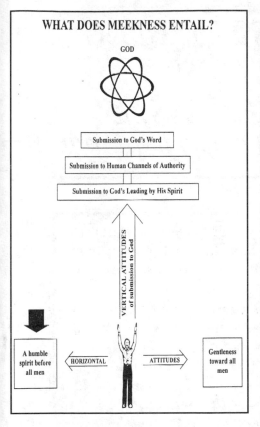

WHAT DOES MEEKNESS ENTAIL?

GOD

Submission to God's Word

Submission to Human Channels of Authority

Submission to God's Leading by His Spirit

VERTICAL ATTITUDES of submission to God

A humble spirit before all men ← HORIZONTAL ATTITUDES → Gentleness toward all men

In the first two sections, we have studied submission from the standpoint of authority, accountability, position, and role in life. As we can see in our diagram, those are the upward or vertical attitudes of meekness towards God.

In this final section, we will look at the outward or horizontal attitudes of meekness toward other people. These are the qualities that Christ's nature within us progressively reflects more and more as we grow in Him.

There are two horizontal qualities involved in meekness—humility and gentleness.

In Mark 8:34, Christ gives the call to discipleship: "If anyone would come after me, he must deny himself and take up his cross and follow me." This call to follow Christ is one of sacrifice. It is a type of submission and self-denial that expresses itself in humility (servitude) and gentleness to other people.

In speaking about self-denial, we do not mean that Christians lose their personal identities. Look at the Apostles. Not one was asked to give up his unique individuality. It is easy to distinguish between the impetuous Peter, the studious and determined Paul, and the quiet but committed Barnabas.

Self-denial means setting aside our own desires and ambitions and submitting our will to Christ. This leads to true fulfillment because Christ said, "whoever...loses his life for me will find it" (Mt. 16:25).

After spending the first 11 chapters explaining all aspects of salvation, in Romans 12:1, Paul says, "*Therefore*, I urge you, brothers, in view of God's mercy, to offer your bodies as living sacrifices, holy and pleasing to God—this is your spiritual act of worship" [emphasis added]. In other words, based on what God has done for us as Christians, we make this sacrifice,

which is the very essence of how we live our life. It is how we bring praise, worship, and glory to God in our daily living.

In humility we sacrificially lay down our lives—our gifts, our talents, and our resources—to serve the needs of others. In gentleness we often sacrifice our own rights to serve the higher law of God's love.

■■■■■■■■■■■■■■■■■■■■■■■■■■■■■■■■

BIBLE STUDY GUIDE

Today's Bible Reading:
Mt. 16:24-25; Ro. 12:1; 1 Pet. 4:10-11

1. What did Jesus say His followers were to do, and what does this mean to you? Mt. 16:24-25 _____

_____

2. How do you relate what Jesus said, to Paul's statement in Romans 12:1?

_____

_____

3. How do you relate what Jesus said, to Peter's statement in 1 Peter 4:10-11? _____

_____

_____

TODAY'S WORLD PRAYER EMPHASIS

MIDDLE EAST - YEMEN
- Population: 16,102,000
- Religion: Muslim 99.9% - Jews 0.02% - Protestant: a few hundred expatriates and a handful of Yemeni secret believers - Catholic 5,000 - Orthodox: Ethiopian refugees
- Needs:
  Yemen was once home to many Christians, but during the Muslim conquest in the time of Muhammed, Yemenis turned from Christianity to Islam. Pray that Jesus Christ will once again take hold of Yemeni hearts.
  Pray for spiritual liberation. The gospel came to Yemen in 1964 when the government asked Christian organizations to set up health care facilities. However, few Yemeni have heard the gospel preached. Pray for a new day of freedom for worship and witness.

HUMILITY'S GREATEST EXAMPLE

In the next few lesson we will look at humility as a quality of meekness. Before we begin, however, we should first look at our greatest example of One who was humble—Jesus Christ.

Jesus communicated the importance of serving others before oneself through everything He taught and did. In Mark 9:35, when the disciples were disputing about who would be the greatest in the kingdom, Christ told them, "If anyone wants to be first, he must be the very last, and the servant of all." Jesus put this teaching into practice throughout His earthly life. For example, in John 13, Jesus lowered Himself to the place of a common slave and washed the feet of His own disciples. When He had done this, He said:

> You call Me 'Teacher' and 'Lord,' and rightly so, for that is what I am. Now that I, your Lord and Teacher, have washed your feet, you should also wash one another's feet. I have set you an example that you should do as I have done for you. I tell you the truth, no servant is greater than his master, nor is a messenger greater than the one who sent him. Now that you know these things, you will be blessed if you do them. (Jn. 13:13-17)

Jesus also demonstrated His willingness to deny Himself society's favor and serve others by His attitude towards women. Even though women were considered little more than property in Jesus' day, He viewed them differently. For example, He spoke to the Samaritan woman at the well—ignoring the social and religious barriers between them—taking time to serve and minister to her spiritual need (Jn. 4:4-29).

Jesus also ministered to children. Children were ranked even lower than women on the social scale. The disciples thought that Jesus was far too important to spend time with the children, but He rebuked them, and gladly took the time to lay His hands upon the little ones and bless them (Mt. 19:13-14).

The ultimate example of Christ's humility and servitude, however, is described in Philippians 2:5-11. In this passage, we read of the incredible condescension of Christ, leaving the realms of glory, taking on the form of humanity, and becoming a servant of all people by giving His life for their salvation. This, of course, shows to the fullest extent the self-denial involved in the Cross.

Jesus took up His cross and suffered there for us, denying Himself that He might serve us. We, in turn, are to take up our cross and lose our life in the service of others.

BIBLE STUDY GUIDE

Today's Bible Reading:
John 13:1-17

1. What did Jesus do for His disciples and what would be your reaction if a king or even a leader of your country offered to do the same thing for you? Jn. 13:4-8 _____

_____

_____

_____

_____

2. What does Jesus teach us about humbling ourselves to serve others? Jn. 13:12-17_____

_____

_____

_____

_____

TODAY'S WORLD PRAYER EMPHASIS

AFRICA - ZAIRE
- Population: 41,813,000
- Religion: Traditional religions 2.7% - Protestant 36% - Roman Catholic 42.1% - Orthodox 0.02% - Marginal 17.8%
- Needs:
  Pray that the Christians in this nation would find true life in Christ. Some 30% of the "Christians" in Zaire no longer attend church.
  Pray that the church will rise up and be a moral witness to this country. In the capital city alone, approximately 20% of the population suffers from the AIDS virus.
  Pray that believers will repent of their corruption and moral permissiveness.
  There is currently an effort to reach the Swahili-speaking Muslim communities all over Zaire. Pray that these efforts will be successful.

AVOIDING SELFISH AMBITION AND VANITY

Christ calls us to walk the same road that He did. As He took up the cross of Calvary and carried it for us, so are we to take up our cross and sacrificially serve others. As He served us and gave us eternal salvation, we must serve the needs of those He brings along our path.

Philippians 2:3-4 tells us to "do nothing out of selfish ambition or vain conceit, but in humility consider others better than yourselves. Each of you should look not only to your own interest, but also to the interests of others."

In this lesson, we will examine our responsibility as Christians in light of these verses.

Above all else, we must avoid doing things only because of what we can get out of it or for self-recognition. Although Jesus was God, He did not act out of the desire to exalt and serve Himself. Rather He set aside His divine glory and took on human form to serve a bruised humanity.

In the same way, we are not to have an ambition that is self-serving or that egotistically exalts "self." Rather, we are to act without any ulterior motive—expecting nothing in return as we sacrificially give to others.

Selfish ambition and vanity are results of the pride-of-life which is very much a part of the world's philosophy and, unfortunately, a part of the church as well. So often, out of selfish ambition we seek a "higher" position in the church rather than recognizing the position in ministry God has given us. When we stoop to competitive office-seeking in the church, the basis for humility is destroyed. This results in strife within the body of Christ.

The Scripture tells us to humble ourselves under God's mighty hand so that He may exalt us in due time. Seeking personal advancement on the basis of selfish ambition and vain conceit is useless. Those who humble themselves under God, however, will be exalted to the positions He has for them in due time (1 Pet. 5:6).

Paul said that true humility is considering others better than ourselves. This does not mean we look down upon or neglect ourselves. Rather Paul says that it means looking "not only to [our] own interests, but also to the interests of others." We must also take care of our own needs, or we will not have the health and strength we need to serve others. Our natural tendency is to want only to serve ourselves. Christianity reverses this desire, but not at the expense of our own psychological and spiritual well being.

Finally, in Philippians 2:5, Paul tells us that our attitudes "should be the same as that of Christ Jesus." We must humble ourselves as Christ did and rescue a hurting world.

Only as we put away our selfish ambitions and vanity and serve others as Christ served us through the Cross, can we rescue the lost and heal their broken hearts.

■■■■■■■■■■■■■■■■■■■■■■■■■■■■■■■■■■■

BIBLE STUDY GUIDE

Today's Bible Reading:
Philippians 2:1-11, 3:3-7; James 3:13-16

1. What does Paul say is the opposite of self-ambition? Phil. 3:3-7 _____

_____

_____

_____

_____

2. Where does James say self-ambition comes from? Jas. 3:13-16_____

_____

_____

_____

_____

TODAY'S WORLD PRAYER EMPHASIS

EUROPE - MACEDONIA
- Population: 2,130,000
- Religion: Non-religious/other 8.3-13.3% - Muslim 25-30% - Protestant 0.18% - Roman Catholic 2.3% - Orthodox 60.3% - Marginal 0.05%
- Needs:
  Pray for ethnic harmony and sensitivity on the part of leaders as they face an uncertain future.
  Pray for the Holy Spirit to bring new life to the Macedonian Orthodox Church. Many Macedonians are bound by superstition.
  Pray for the unreached—the capital, Skopje, and surrounding cities; the large Gypsy population; the Albanian community; and the Turkish community.
  The Macedonian Bible, published in 1988, has been rejected by most Christians as being grossly inaccurate. Pray for the quick completion of the new translation.

CONSIDER OTHERS BETTER THAN YOURSELF

Often, people have a tendency to look down upon others. Quite often this occurs because of one's superior education, income, social position, or position of responsibility. Even in the church this tendency is prevelant.

Most of the time this attitude stems from the pride-of-life mentioned in 1 John 2:16-17.

Yet despite worldly tendencies, Paul tells us that as Christians we must "consider others better than [ourselves]" (Philippians 2:4).

We can see the particular relevance of this exhortation to the church at Philippi. For we are told in Acts 16, that this church had a great diversity of people.

Within the Philippian church was an uneducated slave girl who had performed divination before she was delivered from demons and converted (Acts 16:16-19).

There was also a middle-class jailor. This man was probably a retired Roman soldier and no doubt a Roman citizen (Acts 16:33-34).

In the church was also a wealthy and refined business woman named Lydia (Acts 16:14).

Without doubt, all walks of life attended the Philippian church, just as they attend our churches today. Thus, this passage of Paul in Philippians 2 has as much relevance for us today as it did for the church in that day.

Like Paul, James also warns us against showing partiality in the church on the basis of a person's material wealth. This means we must not show special favors to but a few; rather we must count all as better than ourselves—especially those who may have less of this world's material goods (Jas. 2:1-9).

There is one caution. In considering others better than ourselves we are not to disregard our own affairs. That would be irresponsible both toward God and ourselves. We must include the interests of others within the sphere of our own psychological and physical health.

As we look to the interests of others we will be able to find true fulfillment in life.

In giving of our time and our resources in loving service to others, we discover that those who lose their life for Christ's sake acturally finds it, and we realize that it is more blessed to give than to receive (Matt. 16:25; Acts 20:35).

BIBLE STUDY GUIDE

Today's Bible Reading:
James 2:1-12

1. What does James adamantly tell us we should not do as believers?
Jas. 2:1-4_____

_____

_____

_____

_____

2. When we don't keep the second greatest commandment as it pertains to all people—regardless of class, color, creed, or nationality—what are we doing? Jas. 2:8-11 _____

_____

_____

_____

_____

_____

TODAY'S WORLD PRAYER EMPHASIS

AFRICA - ZIMBABWE
- Population: 11,352,000
- Religion: Traditional religions 32.6% - Non-religious/others 4% - Muslim 1.6% - Protestant 33% - Roman Catholic 12% - Marginal 16.69%
- Needs:
  Praise God for the unprecedented freedom to preach the gospel in public, as well as through various forms of media communications! There has been spectacular growth in the Church due to large evangelistic crusades as well as massive distribution of Christian literature and the Scriptures.
  Pray for the exisitng Church. Even though there has been growth, much of the Church is still stagnate. Pray that they will take a stand against witchcraft and the demonic powers that bind this nation in the name of nationalism and tradition.
  Pray for spiritual unity within the Church so that a strong moral witness can be shown to a nation plagued by death due to AIDS.
  Pray for the less reached—those in rural areas and inner-cities; Muslims; and Mozambican refugees fleeing civil war.

HUMILITY IN LEADERSHIP

The concept of serving one another in humility is a liberating one, particularly for those in positions of leadership.

Without a commitment to this type of servitude, our old nature tends to lord it over those who are placed under us and to demand their involuntary service. This can easily lead to arrogance and intolerance, as well as manipulating and ignoring the needs of those being led. Human beings who are in a lower position of authority in any given situation (school, employment, government, and so forth) can be simply regarded as tools to be used for the accomplishing of the purpose at hand. This leads to the destruction of the self-worth and self-respect of the subordinated individuals involved.

However, leaders who embrace a Christ-like humility and seek to serve those under them become attentive to the needs of their subordinates as persons and seek to minister to them. As a result, their actual authority and effectiveness is greatly enhanced because those who render respect and service to them do it willingly rather than as a result of coercion. A widespread application of Christian humility in various institutions would revolutionize the effectiveness of leaders and the ability to fulfill designated functions.

In the world's eyes, leadership is not just a function. Leaders have a superior status. They are different from the masses. They are not just differently gifted people, they are better people. For this reason, positions of leadership often carry with them prestige and recognition. Indeed, many seek a higher position because of the acclaim and personal power over other people that goes along with being a leader.

The world's view of leadership status is really different than the Christian view. Though Jesus declared that there is a definite role which belongs to the leader who serves Christ, the position of a Christian leader is certainly not the pedestal upon which the world places leaders.

The diagram shown distinguishes between how the world views the status and function of a leader and how Christ views it.

We see clearly that the one who would exercise leadership in Christ's kingdom, or in society, must, in fact, be a servant.

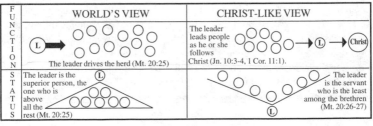

110

BIBLE STUDY GUIDE

Today's Bible Reading:
Matthew 25:34-40; Mark 10:42-45

1. What should every person who is a Christian be doing, and how do you think this relates especially to those who lead? Mt. 25:35-36_____

_____

_____

_____

_____

_____

2. What is happening when we minister to the needs of people? Mt. 25:37-40 _____

_____

_____

3. What did Jesus say about those who are "first," or have high positions of leadership? Mk. 10:42-45 _____

_____

_____

_____

TODAY'S WORLD PRAYER EMPHASIS

EUROPE - ALBANIA
- Population: 3,521,000
- Religion: Non-religious/other 41.9% - Muslim 40% - Baha'i 0.12% - Protestant 0.06% - Roman Catholic 7% - Orthodox 10.9% - Marginal 0.02%
- Needs:

   Praise God for the changes taking place in Albania! Religion is now openly encouraged as an antidote to the crime epidemic that came with the spread of freedom.

   Pray for wisdom for the leaders of this nation as they make the transition to a democratic/capitalistic state. Pray that they will act in moderation to the ethnic difficulties that have occured in the face of freedom.

   Many religions from all over the world seek to establish strong churches in Albania. As wonderful as this may seem for Christianity, it can be very dangerous as more and more mysticism and cultic practices take root. Pray that the spirit of deception will be bound and that Albanians will find the true way to God through Jesus Christ.

WEEKEND DEVOTIONAL GUIDE

1. *Your prayer needs:*

• *Each week write down your newest prayer requests.*
• *After praying over them, transfer them to your main* God is Faithful
Prayer List *on page 162 and remember them daily.*
• *Each time a request is answered, draw a red line through it and date it
at the end.*

2. *Crossroads Christian Communications Prayer Need*

Pray for Crossroads' partners, that God will bless them, protect their
families, and draw any unsaved loved ones to Himself.

3. *Lay Leadership International Prayer Need*

Pray for Carol Hill as she works with Don. She asks especially that
you pray for the efforts to recruit more people into the LLI Interces-
sory Prayer Ministry.

WEEKEND JOURNAL

Thoughts to reflect on and record:

1. Do I know what my cross, or call to service, is? Am I making the kind of sacrifice it requires?

2. Are there pockets of pride in me that would keep me from humbling myself and serving certain people in certain levels of society?

3. In my desire to succeed or have something, do I view others as what they can do for me rather than as what I can do for them? Do I put people's needs before my own desires?

4. Am I accepting of all people, regardless of their position in life? Is there any type of person that I look down upon? Like Jesus, would I go and associate with questionable people regardless of the social pressure inside or outside the church not to do so?

5. In matters of business, am I concerned about the needs of the other person or persons, even though I may have to take less profit for myself?

HUMILITY IN THE FAMILY

The same principles of leadership shown in the diagram in lesson 45 apply to leadership in the family.

The person in authority is called to serve, not to lord their position over the other members of the family.

God's model for the Christian home requires submission by both the wife and the husband.

The husband is to love his wife as Christ loves the Church. This means that he is called in humility to surrender to a life of self-denial. He is constantly to be considerate of his wife's total needs as a person.

In most cultures, husbands are not prepared for this type of humble submission. Instead, the dominant partner often sees his authority as an excuse to have his own way and ignore the needs of his wife.

Wives are told to submit to their husbands in everything as to the Lord. For the Scriptures state that the husband is the head of the wife even as Christ is head of the Church (Eph. 5:22-24).

However, the attitude and principle of submission is not one-sided. For we see that when Paul begins his discussion of the relationship with regard to authority between husbands and wives, he starts out with the remark, "Submit to one another out of reverence to Christ" (Eph. 5:21).

The husband is not called to surrender his role of leadership at home. However, as part of his position, he is called to submit himself in humility to the task of fulfilling the needs and desires of his spouse, caring for her with the same love and attention Christ has for His church (Eph. 5:22-28).

We often understand and act out this principle of submission and service in relation to our children more than we do in relation to our spouse. Although it is very important to take care of the needs of our children, meeting the needs of our spouse is even more vital. For this spousal relationship is at the very core of the family. Without this relationship it is almost impossible to meet the needs of the children.

In the area of training and instruction, parents are called to exercise authority over their children. Likewise, the Scriptures teach that children are to honor and obey their parents (Eph. 6:1-4).

Parents go to great lengths to meet their children's needs—even after their children become adults. Yet how often we find those same parents neglecting to submit to their spouse (whether husband or wife) out of the love Christ has given them for that person. When there is submission to each other, however, there develops a cord of love in their relationship that binds the family together—a bond which can never be broken.

BIBLE STUDY GUIDE

Today's Bible Reading:
Ephesians 5:21-32; 1 Peter 3:1-7

1. What does Paul say every person is to do? Eph. 5:21 _____
_____
_____

2. What are wives asked to do, and what does this mean to you?
Eph. 5:22-24; 1 Pet. 3:1-6_____
_____
_____
_____
_____

3. What are husbands asked to do, and what does this mean to you?
Eph. 5:25-32; 1 Pet. 3:7_____
_____
_____
_____
_____

TODAY'S WORLD PRAYER EMPHASIS

ASIA - BANGLADESH
- Population: 132,219,000
- Religion: Muslim 87% - Hindu 11.7% - Buddhist 0.6% - Other 0.3% - Protestant 0.44% - Roman Catholic 0.21%
- Needs:
  Pray that freedom of religion will be preserved in the face of Islamic pressures.
  Pray for the unreached people—the Muslims, who number 100 million; the Hindus, who have been strongly resistant to the gospel; the Bihari, Muslim refugees who have refused Bangladeshi citizenship and have been denied entry into India and Pakistan; the Rohingya Muslims, refugees from Myanmar; the tribal peoples; and for students, young people, and children.
  Pray for distribution of the Scriptures, as well as Christian media outreaches—i.e., radio outreaches, the *Jesus* film; and audiocassette ministries.

HUMILITY IN THE CHURCH

One of the most important areas in which humility must be exercised is in the church. Leadership of the church—pastors, elders, deacons, and so forth—means above all else, serving those who are being led.

1 Peter 5:2-3 teaches that elders should,

> Tend—nurture, guard, guide the fold—the flock of God that is [your responsibility], not by coercion *or* constraint but willingly; not dishonorably, motivated by the advantages *and* profits [belonging to the office], but eagerly *and* cheerfully. Not [as arrogant, dictatorial, and overbearing persons] domineering over those in your charge, but being examples—patterns and models of Christian living—to the flock (the congregation). (AB)

In the author's opinion, most factions in the local church evolve when there is a lack of surrender to this humble Spirit of Christ on the part of each member. Elders have a much graver responsibility than the general membership to demonstrate this humble spirit to the world.

Likewise, the younger leaders of the church are to submit to the leadership of the elders and also serve in humility. 1 Peter 5:5-6 says,

> Likewise you that are younger *and* of lesser rank be subject to the elders—the ministers and spiritual guides of the church, giving them due respect and yielding to their counsel. Clothe (apron) yourselves, all of you, with humility—as the garb of a servant, so that its covering cannot possibly be stripped from you, with freedom from pride and arrogance—toward one another. For God sets Himself against the proud—the insolent, the overbearing, the disdainful, the presumptuous, the boastful, and opposes, frustrates and defeats them—but gives grace (favor, blessing) to the humble. [Prov. 3:34.]
>
> Therefore, humble yourselves (demote, lower yourselves in your own estimation) under the mighty hand of God, that in due time He may exalt you. (AB)

Finally, and very importantly, members are to submit to leadership. Hebrews 13:17 says,

> Obey your spiritual leaders and submit to them—continually recognizing their authority over you; for they are constantly keeping watch over your souls *and* guarding your spiritual welfare, as men who will have to render an account [of their trust]. [Do your part to] let them do this with gladness, and not with sighing *and* groaning, for that would not be profitable to you [either]. (AB)

The Scripture makes it very plain that members of a local church are to submit to the leaders God has given them. As was emphasized in a previous lesson, there is a definite authority structure in the church and God expects us to submit in humility to those He has placed over us.

Therefore, humility in the Church is a two-way street. Both those who lead and those who follow are called to serve.

■■■■■■■■■■■■■■■■■■■■■■■■■■■■■■■■■■■■■

BIBLE STUDY GUIDE
Today's Bible Reading:
Hebrews 13:17; 1 Peter 5:1-6

1. What do spiritual leaders do for us? Heb. 13:17 _____

_____

_____

_____

_____

2. How are spiritual leaders supposed to lead? 1 Pet. 5:1-4_____

_____

_____

_____

3. What does Peter tell the young leaders to do? 1 Pct. 5:5-6 _____

_____

_____

_____

TODAY'S WORLD PRAYER EMPHASIS

EUROPE - AUSTRIA
- Population: 7,479,000
- Religion: Non-religious/other 8.2% - Muslim 1.4% - Jewish 0.08% - Baha'i 0.02% - Buddhist 0.01% - Protestant 5.3% - Roman Catholic 83% - Other Catholic 0.33% Orthodox 0.94% - Marginal 0.74%
- Needs:

  Though a nation known for music, art, and beauty, high rates of suicide, abortion, and alcoholism belie a great spiritual need in Austria. Pray that this nation will be set free by the power of Jesus Christ.

  Pray for the less-reached people of this nation—those in the provinces; those in the small towns; and especially those bound by cultic religions.

  Crossroads has helped train Austrians for Christian television production. They have been telecasting on an Italian border station in an Austrian television network. Pray that their programs will bear fruit for the Kingdom.

HUMILITY IN THE WORLD

Christians are called to serve the needs of their neighbors through acts of kindness and sharing. They are to submit to the needs of the community by giving themselves in service as a member of the body of Christ. The Bible calls us to minister to the broken and despised, to stoop to the lowest and the downtrodden, to identify with them, and to help them (Mt. 25:31-46). This willingness to submit to the needs of others as we encounter them along life's way is the central theme of the Parable of the Good Samaritan (Lk. 10:24-37). The Christian must determine to live as a responsible person in an increasingly irresponsible world.

Such responsibility places a great deal of biblical accountability upon Christians who lead in the marketplace. Leaders in business or in various areas of society—professional, academics, and so forth—are called by God to serve the people under them. For instance, for the Christian business owner, it may mean using some of the profits to help facilitate meeting the needs of employees. The Christian witness requires going beyond what the rules of government stipulate concerning employer/employee relationships. The real issue is: *How can I sacrificially serve those God has given me influence over?* Granted, Christian business leaders are somewhat constrained by all the concerns of business—economics, profits, etc.—and can only do what they are able. But, when conditions are favorable, God asks of those who lead in the marketplace to be motivated by God's kingdom and be concerned for people. They are not to be motivated by greed or simply for personal gain.

Likewise, for Christian professionals it may mean giving free quality service in their area of expertise to those who cannot afford it. The majority of the people in the world are poor. These are the people for whom Christ had great compassion because He saw them being harassed and helpless, like sheep without a shepherd (Mt. 9:36). He instructed His disciples to have compassion for those people also (Lk. 10:2).

In this same portion of scripture, Christ also prayed for laborers. These are laborers that come from every level and spectrum of society. Each person who serves Christ has his or her calling and responsibility to humbly meet the needs of others who are hurting.

The illustrations of how to meekly serve Christ in the marketplace are too numerous to mention. Yet in all cases, how we, as Christians, minister to people is how they will see Jesus Christ. Our meek behavior is often one of the beams of light that draws people to accept Christ as their personal Lord and Savior.

BIBLE STUDY GUIDE

Today's Bible Reading:
Matthew 9:35-38; Acts 10:38

1. When Jesus looked on the people of His day, what did He see? Do you think the situation is any different today? Mt. 9:35-36 _____

_____

_____

_____

2. What was Christ calling His disciples to do? Do you think that call applies to every believer or just a certain few? Mt. 9:37-38 _____

_____

_____

3. In Acts 10:38, how did the Disciples explain the two-fold ministry of Jesus Christ? How do you relate Christ's ministry to what He was calling people to do in Matthew 9:35-38?_____

_____

_____

_____

TODAY'S WORLD PRAYER EMPHASIS

ASIA - BHUTAN
- Population: 671,000
- Religion: Lamaistic Buddhist 70.1% - Hindu 24% - Muslim 5% - Protestant 0.25% Roman Catholic 0.08%
- Needs:
  Pray that this land will be further opened to the gospel. Restrictions were lessened in 1965. However, due to an increase in Christianity, more restrictions have now been put into place.
  Christians have been allowed to operate leprosy hospitals, agricultural and educational programs, and so forth on the condition that they do not proselytize. Pray that the Lord will use these ministries not only to reach the people who use them, but also as a witness to the government so that more doors will be opened for missionaries to enter the country.

BEING GENTLE

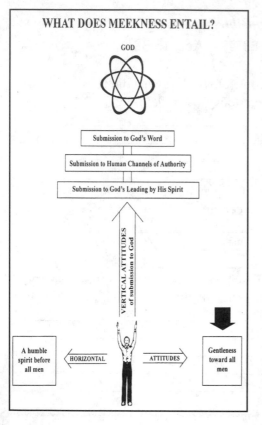

WHAT DOES MEEKNESS ENTAIL?

GOD

Submission to God's Word

Submission to Human Channels of Authority

Submission to God's Leading by His Spirit

VERTICAL ATTITUDES
of submission to God

A humble spirit before all men ← HORIZONTAL ATTITUDES → Gentleness toward all men

Like humility, the concept of gentleness toward all people is also a type of submission. It means giving up our personal rights to serve the higher law of God's love. Before we can demonstrate this horizontal attitude of gentleness toward people, we must first cultivate the vertical attitude of meekness toward God.

As we studied in previous lessons, this attitude entails submission to God's Word, His human channels of authority, and the leading of the Holy Spirit. Only as we cultivate meekness toward God in these areas can we demonstrate meekness toward others in our daily lives. If our relationship with God is not right, then how we relate to others will be adversely affected.

In Matthew 5:38-42 and Luke 6:27-36, we have an exposition on the very essence of meekness and gentleness by our Lord Himself. Gentleness toward everyone as Jesus lived and taught it is contrary to the wisdom of this world. Our carnal nature reacts in a negative way to a lifestyle that seeks to not claim one's own rights. There is a part of our being that asks, *"Why should we love our enemies and allow ourselves to be taken advantage of? Why should we give what is ours and not demand it back*? The answer is quite simple: *This is the essence of true love.* True love gives and demands nothing in return. It even gives to those who show no appreciation for its sacrifices nor any desire to repay that which was shared freely.

True love is evident in our lives when we can love the unlovable; when we can love without expecting anything in return; and when we can love others as freely as God loves us. We find the ultimate example of true love in the gospel: "This is love: not that we love God, but that he loved us and sent his Son as an atoning sacrifice for our sins" (1 Jn. 4:10).

Gentleness is the outward display of true love. Gentleness treats the other person properly, even when there's nothing in return. When we have cultivated our vertical relationship with God, gentleness becomes an outward manifestation of His love for us and the rest of the world.

■■■■■■■■■■■■■■■■■■■■■■■■■■■■■■■■

BIBLE STUDY GUIDE
Today's Bible Reading:
Ephesians 4:1-6; Colossians 3:12-13

1. What is one of the things we can do to walk as worthy believers of Jesus Christ? Eph. 4:1-2 _____ _____

_____

_____

2. How are Christians to clothe themselves? Col. 3:12-13_____ _____

_____

_____

TODAY'S WORLD PRAYER EMPHASIS

AFRICA - BURKINA FASO
- Population: 10,382,000
- Religion: Traditional religions 33% - Muslim 48% - Protestant 5% - Roman Catholic 13.9% - Marginal 0.12%
- Needs:
  Praise God for growth in the evangelical church! Membership doubled between 1983 and 1990.

  Pray for the unreached peoples—the Muslims whose population continues to grow within every ethnic group; the Fulani, a partly nomadic people who are just beginning to be reached; and the non-Muslim peoples in various tribes who are still plagued by the fear that is entrenched in their traditional tribal religions.

  Pray for ministry outreaches to the young people in this nation, most of whom are better educated than their parents. Because of local job prospects being so poor, many are frustrated and disillusioned.

  Some years agao, Crossroads provided aid through a wonderful Canadian Christian mission known as the Nazinga Project. Please pray for the continued conversion of the people to Christ and for the establishment of more churches.

WHO SAID GENTLENESS IS EASY?

In this lesson we are going to look at what Jesus said in the Sermon on the Mount about gentleness towards people, especially our enemies. We are going to also contrast what Jesus taught with how society's values usually say we should react.

Although sometimes situations we face can be complex and the direction God is leading may seem especially difficult to follow, the words of Jesus should always make us stop and deeply consider the course of our actions. We should ask ourselves: *In these situations, what will happen if I choose to serve the higher law of love? Am I willing to trust that God will give back to me when I give to my enemy as Luke 6:38 indicates?*

In Matthew 5:38-42, Jesus teaches us to live contrary to the world's thinking. Though the world cries for retribution and retaliation when one is wronged, Jesus said not to avenge oneself in any way—turn the other cheek and forgive as often as is necessary (verse 38).

The ways of the world also teaches us to fight to keep our possessions. Yet Jesus says to give the people what they want and more, "And if someone wants to sue you and take your tunic, let him have your cloak as well" (verse 40). He tells us that our security and preservation are in the hands of God.

Our human inclination is to always do our own thing—we are determined not to let anyone violate our personal liberties and force us to do something we don't want to do.

Yet in verse 41, Jesus taught that Christians are to yield to the unfair pressure and actually do more than the world requires of them.

These lessons were as unusual and radical in Jesus' time as they are today. Yet He not only taught them, but willingly exemplified them through His daily living as well.

Again in Luke 6:27-36, Christ teaches that not only are Christians not to retaliate against their enemies, but they are to go a step further and pray for them. Jesus teaches that even people of the world love those who love them. But God demands a higher standard. Christians are to "Love those who do not love you—those you consider your enemies" (Lk. 6:35).

Gentleness, especially when shown towards an enemy, often relies on our willingness to trust in God's plan, even though we rarely fully understand it. Yet as the Holy Spirit works within us to develop gentle attitudes, we will reflect this Christ-like attitude to the world and they will be drawn to Him.

BIBLE STUDY GUIDE
Today's Bible Reading:
Matthew 5:38-42; Luke 6:27-38

1. List the things Christ tells us to do to our enemies. Do you think it's possible to live as He says? Mt. 5:38-42; Lk. 6:27-31 _____

_____

_____

_____

_____

2. If we trust Christ by not fighting or resisting our enemies, what does He promise? Lk. 6:38 _____

_____

_____

_____

TODAY'S WORLD PRAYER EMPHASIS

ASIA - BRUNEI
- Population: 301,000
- Religion: Muslim 71% - Chinese Religions 9% - Non-religious/other 6.5% - Animist/other faiths 5.5% - Protestant 3.8% - Roman Catholic 3.9% - Marginal 0.21%
- Needs:

  No evangelism is permitted within the Muslim community which has no known believers within it. However, there is a steady stream of conversions from Islam among the tribal and immigrant communities. Pray that Christians may witness to these people by living pure lives and that through the work of the Holy Spirit some may be saved.

  The Chinese community still feels very unaccepted in this nation. Many follow traditional Chinese religions, while some are nominal Christians. Pray that fear and materialistic concerns will not hold back the Chinese from salvation.

  Pray for Christians undergoing a religious apartheid to be strengthened. In 1992, the importation of Christian literature and the public celebration of Christmas were banned, and all contacts with Christians outside of the country were banned as well. Pray also that these edicts, which are unconstitutional by the standards of Brunei, will be removed.

WEEKEND DEVOTIONAL GUIDE

1. *Your prayer needs:*

• *Each week write down your newest prayer requests.*
• *After praying over them, transfer them to your main* God is Faithful
Prayer List *on page 162 and remember them daily.*
• *Each time a request is answered, draw a red line through it and date it
at the end.*

2. *Crossroads Christian Communications Prayer Need*

Pray for local churches and their continued relationship with Crossroads in reaping the harvest for God.

3. *Lay Leadership International Prayer Need*

Pray for LLI's outreach to local churches. Pray that God will help
many pastors embrace a more complete approach to equipping and
discipling people for service ministries.

WEEKEND JOURNAL

Thoughts to reflect on and record:

1. How do my views of the role of a husband or wife measure up to what I understand the Bible to be saying?

2. Being raised and educated in a highly individualistic society, am I a person who subjects myself to God's authority in the Church?

3. Do I view myself as a co-laborer with Christ, having compassion for a world of people harassed by Satan? In what ways can I help continue the ministry of Jesus mentioned in Acts 10:38?

4. Have I ever been involved in situations where I do not handle fellow believers or others with the gentleness and compassion of Jesus Christ?

5. When I get caught in a situation where people become my enemies, am I ready to respond in the gentleness of Christ? Am I willing to trust and obey God and do what Jesus said, believing that He will give back to me as He promised in Luke 6:38?

NON-RETALIATION IS REVOLUTIONARY

Because non-retaliation is such a revolutionary concept and runs counter to the values in our society, we must take a closer look at it.

In Luke 6:27, what did Jesus really mean when He said, "*love your enemies*"? He meant that we are to love those who for some reason or another may even hate us. This revolutionary idea is precisely what Jesus brings out in the Parable of the Good Samaritan. The Jew who was beaten by the thieves and left to die represented the entire race of Jews who despised and hated the Samaritans just as much as the Samaritans despised and hated the Jews. Both races continually demonstrated social prejudice of the worst kind. Yet the Good Samaritan chose not to retaliate by leaving the Jewish man to die. Rather he chose to show love and mercy to the one who was his enemy and he bestowed upon the Jew many acts of kindness.

In Luke 6:28, Jesus says to bless those who curse you and to pray for those who mistreat you. In verse 30, Christ tells us not to withhold benevolence because someone hates you or has treated you wrongly, rather, if you can, give to everyone you encounter who has a need. Always treat others as you would want to be treated, regardless of how they have treated you in the past.

This teaching is very difficult for us to accept and act upon because it opposes what society has taught us. Sometimes, when we are not treating our neighbors well, we want to justify ourselves much like the lawyer in Luke 6:32-33 by asking, "But who is my neighbor?" Christ tells us that our neighbor is not necessarily our friend, but rather anyone we come into contact with who has a need. Jesus reminds us that it's easy to treat friends right, especially if they reciprocate our kindness as good friends do. However, those who are meek give, not because of what they expect in return, but because they possess Christ's love for others.

When Christians lend (that is, give) to a person in need, like the Good Samaritan, they expect nothing in return. It is interesting, however, that Jesus used the word *lend* instead of *give*. He did so because even though the meek do not expect it, there is a reward. As the *Living Bible* says in Proverbs 19:17, "When you help the poor, you are lending to the Lord—and he pays wonderful interest on your loan." When we give expecting nothing in return from those whose needs we serve, then our reward will be great.

When we choose to react with gentle love and non-retaliation toward everyone (including our enemies), we will be called children of the Most High (Lk. 26:35-36). This is one of the great ways we reflect the image of God to others.

BIBLE STUDY GUIDE

Today's Bible Reading:
Luke 10:25-37

Today our Bible study approach will be somewhat different. In light of our Bible reading, try and analyze how you would feel in a similar situation.

1. If you knew a person was in great need, but they were part of a group of people who looked down on you, held you back, or had performed numerous injustices toward you and your family, how would you react to thier need?_____

_____

_____

2. If this person represented a group that had plundered your every opportunity for success, would you give money to meet their need?_____

_____

_____

3. Think of a person in real life who has done an injustice to you in the past. Would you help them when they're down?_____

_____

_____

TODAY'S WORLD PRAYER EMPHASIS

NORTH AMERICA - CANADA
- Population: 27,567,000
- Religion: Non religious/other 12.1% - Non-Christian religions 4.4% - Protestant 32.2% - Roman Catholic 45.2% - Other Catholic 0.8% - Orthodox 2.9% Marginal 2.4%
- Needs:
  For 32 years, Crossroads has been sowing the good seed of the Word of God through television across Canada. Please water that seed daily with your prayers. We have the promise from the Lord that He will cause it to grow.

  The evangelical witness in Canada has declined steadily through this century. Pray that evangelical Christians may break out of their isolationism and unite to make an impact on this nation in this hour of spiritual need.

WHY BE HUMBLE AND GENTLE?

As disciples of Christ, we must begin to identify with God's unfathomable love for the human race. As we do this, we begin to comprehend His wonderful but costly plan of redemption, and the sacrifices that may be required of us to flow in harmony with that plan.

Christ sacrificially set aside His high and rightful place in heaven to redeem all people and bring them back to the Father's original intention for them—that they might glorify Him.

In the same way, we must be willing to surrender our rights and sacrificially serve others in meekness so that we can draw them to the Father by demonstrating His love to them (Jn. 3:16).

Jesus said, "I have come down from heaven not to do my own will but to do the will of him who sent me" (Jn. 6:38).

Jesus demonstrated perfect meekness in submitting Himself to the Father's plan. He knew full well that this plan entailed not only a life of humble service among the people, but also the degrading and painful humiliation of the cross.

He did not shrink from these tasks, however. Rather, He gave up all His rights and literally lost His life in order to serve God's eternal love and purpose.

As we truly meditate upon this costly love of Christ and His meekness, we are motivated to likewise serve others in meekness.

The call to discipleship is a call of self-giving love. It is a call to give up everything for Christ's sake (Mt. 16:25). This is what Christ meant when He told us to deny ourselves and take up our cross and follow Him.

To take up our cross is to lose our life in the service of others. Yet, in so doing, we find a life filled with His abundance. True fulfillment comes as we immerse ourselves in ministry to others.

Again, we must emphasize that this does not mean we do not take care of our own needs. We must take care of ourselves so that we can serve our neighbors more effectively.

As we allow the Holy Spirit to work within us and make us more and more like Christ, we will become better examples of His love and compassion to others—even our enemies.

BIBLE STUDY GUIDE

Today's Bible Reading:
Romans 15:1-4

1. When we encounter people who are in a state of weakness, what should we do? Ro. 15:1-2 _____

_____

_____

_____

_____

_____

2. What did Christ do when confronted by insulting people? Ro. 15:3_____

_____

_____

_____

_____

TODAY'S WORLD PRAYER EMPHASIS

EUROPE - CROATIA
• Population: 4,832,000
• Religion: Non-religious/other 6.8% - Muslim est. 5% - Protestants 0.6% - Roman Catholic 72.5% - Other Catholic 0.16% - Orthodox 14.8% - Marginal 0.15%
• Needs:
  Pray for a recent Croatian graduate of Crossroads' Dr. Geoffrey R. Conway School of Broadcasting. Pray that doors will open to share the gospel on Croatian television.
  Pray for reconciliation between the Serbs and Croats. Past atrocities on both sides have to be faced if a lasting peace is to be attained. Only through Christ can such a reconciliation be achieved.

LOVE ALWAYS WINS

In difficult situations, we often wonder whether the love of God will truly be of help, especially when our human inclination is to fight for what we have. However, 1 Corinthians 14:1 tells us, "Let love be your greatest aim" (TLB).

During the Crusades, men tried to convert the world through force. History reveals that the Crusades certainly did not succeed. In fact, in most situations they had the exact opposite effect. People were turned against these so-called Christians who burned their cities and killed their neighbors.

Just as the Crusades failed to convert men and women to Christ many centuries ago, so will our efforts to win people for the Kingdom fail unless they are done in the spirit of meekness and love.

Trying to win people through a gospel of fear or pressure is simply not God's way. The Bible says that the meek will inherit the earth. God's way to victory is meekness. God's way to victory is love (Mt. 5:5).

In 1 Corinthians 13, the apostle Paul gives a beautiful picture of the selfless love that God requires of us. Paul tells us that all the spiritual gifts and all the good works in the world are worthless unless they are exercised in love.

Let us look at the description of love this scripture so beautifully gives. We see that the love of Christ that dwells within His people is always considerate of others. It displays patience and kindness, while shunning jealousy, boasting arrogance, and rudeness.

This love does not always want its own way. It is never bad-tempered or hard to get along with. Nor does it hold grudges.

It is saddened by sin and happy when right prevails and truth is presented. Love puts up with anything. It never ceases to trust in God or believe in a bright future.

Love never gives up, nor will it pass away.

We see that our limited and imperfect gifts of knowledge will not endure. For one day they will be set aside as we enter into new fullness of understanding in God.

Love, however, will always be central to our lives.

Faith, hope, and love will endure forever, but *the greatest truth of eternity will be love*. (1 Cor. 13:1-13.)

We can be assured that God's love never fails. His love is not forceful or retaliatory. And it is this great love that will ultimately bring all people, even those who persecute us, to Christ.

BIBLE STUDY GUIDE
Today's Bible Reading:
1 Corinthians 13:1-13

1. List all of the things a person can do yet still not exhibit the fruit of the Spirit which is love. 1 Cor. 3:1-3 _____

_____

_____

_____

_____

2. List the qualities of a loving person. 1 Cor. 13:4-7 _____

_____

_____

_____

_____

3. The fruit of the Spirit can be summed up in one word. What is more important than anything else in your Christian walk? 1 Cor. 13:13 _____

_____

TODAY'S WORLD PRAYER EMPHASIS

ASIA - CHINA
- Population: 1,214,221,000
- Religion: Non-religious/other 59.1% - Chinese religions 27% - Buddhist 3% - Animist 2.4% - Muslim 2.4% - Protestant 5.1% - Roman Catholic 0.77% - Marginal 0.18%
- Needs:

  The door in China is open for airing a Chinese translation of Crossroads' *Kingdom Adventure* series. Pray that the Holy Spirit will cause the people to understand the presentation of the gospel in parable form. Pray also for the Chinese long-range television production produced at the Crossroads Centre for the Chinese community in Canada and abroad.

  Pray for Christian families in China to be a light and example to everyone, even in the face of mockery, discrimination, and the constant barage of atheistic propaganda.

THE LAW OF SOWING AND REAPING

Another reason we can be assured the way of meekness and love will always triumph is because of the law of sowing and reaping. Galatians 6:7-10 says,

> Do not be deceived: God cannot be mocked. A man reaps what he sows. The one who sows to please his sinful nature, from that nature will reap destruction; the one who sows to please the Spirit, from the Spirit will reap eternal life. Let us not become weary in doing good, for at the proper time we will reap a harvest if we do not give up. Therefore, as we have opportunity, let us do good to all people, especially to those who belong to the family of believers.

It is for this reason that we need not become weary in doing good, for we can be assured that in due time we will reap a harvest both here and in eternity.

Keep in mind that love is to be our sole motivation. We do not serve others for the purpose of reaping a benefit; that would be wrong. But Jesus said if we seek the Kingdom first, all the things we need will be added to us. It will come to us, even without our asking.

In Luke 6:38, Christ said, "Give, and it will be given to you. A good measure, pressed down, shaken together and running over, will be poured into your lap. For with the measure you use, it will be measured to you."

This verse is often quoted in relation to the giving of money. The truth of God's blessing upon faithful financial stewardship is very biblical. However, in its context, this passage means that God will multiply back to us many times the riches of love and life as we constantly reach out in love to others—especially our enemies.

As we mentioned briefly in lesson 52, if we take up our cross to follow Christ and constantly pour our lives into others, we will experience true and lasting fulfillment. This is because of the law of sowing and reaping. If we sow works of meekness and love, then no matter how people treat us, we will reap fulfillment in life. If, on the other hand, we selfishly hold back our time, money, love, and kindness, we will end up anxious, unhappy, and unfulfilled.

Everyone, at one time or another, has experienced an overwhelming feeling of goodness and contentment when they have done something good for another human being. Some may interpret this experience as a compensation for guilt feelings. It is, rather, the immediate fulfillment of the law of sowing and reaping. It is the result of giving ourselves in humility and love to the needs of others. Hence, the meaning of Luke 6:38 becomes clear: "Give life and it will be given back to you many times over" (paraphrased).

BIBLE STUDY GUIDE

Today's Bible Reading:
Luke 6:38; Galatians 6:7-10

1. How can I be assured that not claiming my rights, acting in love to those who have hurt me, and being gentle will always work out to be the best way? Gal. 6:7-10 _____

_____

_____

_____

2. What does God say He will do for those who are non-retaliatory or non-vindictive in their actions? Lk. 6:38 _____

_____

_____

_____

_____

_____

TODAY'S WORLD PRAYER EMPHASIS

CARIBBEAN - DOMINICA
- Population: 87,000
- Religion: Non-religious/other 8% - Protestant 17% - Roman Catholic 74.2% Marginal 0.8%
- Needs:
  Pray that the Carib Indians—the only surviving indigenous peoples to the Caribbean—may find a living faith in Jesus Christ. They are currently living on an isolated reservation on the northeast coast of Dominica.
  Pray for a greater unity among the Dominican Evangelicals. The majority of the population is nominally Catholic. However, holy living is rare. Pray that the faithful Christians can be a positive moral influence on others.

HOW WE LIVE *IS* IMPORTANT

We hope that one of the things you have gleaned from our study on meekness is that the witness of our lifestyle is equally as important as what we say.

Matthew 5:16 says, "Let your light shine before men, that they may see your good deeds and praise your Father in heaven." As we display humility and gentleness toward everyone, serving them in love, they will see Jesus Christ in us and be drawn to Him.

To remind ourselves of what our witness entails, let's quickly review the points we have covered in our study of meekness.

The world must see Christians as a people under authority. Also, every believer, regardless of their position, must humble themselves and submit to serving others—especially those who have been placed under their authority.

We must never act out of selfish ambition. Rather, we must always consider others better than ourselves. And we must look to their interests as well as our own.

It is particularly important for those in leadership—whether in the world, home , or church—to exemplify such humility by serving those under them. Specifically, leaders in the Church are called to lead the flock in humility, setting the example in loving service to all people.

Just as important as humility, gentleness toward everyone requires giving up our personal rights to serve the higher law of God's love.

It is very difficult to comprehend the true meaning of gentleness, let alone practice it. Turning the other cheek and loving those who mistreat us is completely contrary to the world's philosophy. However, we are motivated to this type of meekness by our supreme love for God and His eternal plan, and by our personal call as a disciple to become like Christ.

Finally, we can be assured that meekness will succeed because love always wins. In every situation, love will prevail—love never fails.

We must also realize that the fulfillment of God's promises will become very evident in our lives because of the fixed law of sowing and reaping. The more we give, even to our enemies, the more we will know true fulfillment ourselves.

Ultimately, meekness is an outward manifestation of God's love. It is impossible to have His love within us without it impacting the way we live and relate to others.

BIBLE STUDY GUIDE

Today's Bible Reading:

Matthew 5:1-16

1. List the qualities that a Christian must exhibit to be a true light of God's grace to the world. Mt. 5:3-11 _____

_____

_____

_____

_____

_____

_____

_____

_____

_____

_____

_____

TODAY'S WORLD PRAYER EMPHASIS

AFRICA - COMORO ISLANDS
- Population: 509,000
- Religion: Muslim 98% - Non-religious/other 1.4% - Protestant 0.16% - Roman Catholic 0.46%
- Needs:

  Before 1973, there had been no evangelization in the islands. The islanders are strong Muslims, but they also practice the occult and spirit possession. Even today open Christian witness is expressly forbidden. Pray that God will bless the current evangelistic efforts, and that He will open the doors for the gospel to be proclaimed publicly.

  The quiet witness of some Christian medical and veterinary workers has won credit and public recognition, as well as to give them opportunity to speak with the islanders. Pray for continued opportunities to witness and that such witnessing will bear fruit.

WEEKEND DEVOTIONAL GUIDE

1. *Your prayer needs:*

• *Each week write down your newest prayer requests.*
• *After praying over them, transfer them to your main* God is Faithful
Prayer List *on page 162 and remember them daily.*
• *Each time a request is answered, draw a red line through it and date it
at the end.*

2. *Crossroads Christian Communications Prayer Need*

Pray for those who have found the Lord through the various Crossroads outreaches, that they will become involved in a local church for
their continued spiritual fellowship and growth.

3. *Lay Leadership International Prayer Need*

Pray for LLI's outreact to Australia under the direction of Henry
Betschel. Pray that the *Life by Design* series will also be aired in
Australia.

WEEKEND JOURNAL

Thoughts to reflect on and record:

1. Do I hold bitterness against, or refuse to forgive, anyone? Do I dislike someone so much for their action toward me that I just couldn't help them if they had a need?

2. If a person who is weak in their understanding of the Scriptures is offended by my actions, am I strong enough in Christ to not please myself, but rather adjust when necessary so as to not offend the person?

3. Are there areas in my life that I need to allow the Holy Spirit to expose and work on? Am I used and involved in some of the things mentioned in 1 Corinthians 13:1-3, and yet still lacking in areas of exhibiting love?

4. In a society that talks so much about knowing and claiming your rights, am I really open to not claiming my "rights" if and when the opportunity arises?

5. As I re-read the Beatitudes, am I open to God continuing to further develop these Christ-like qualities in me?

SPIRITUAL HUNGER:
The Essential Motivation of Discipleship

"Blessed are those who hunger and thirst for righteousness, for they will be filled" (Mt. 5:6).

As we reach the conclusion of this final section, we are going to look at the fourth Beatitude. It may seem strange that only now are we examining that which is at the very core of the disciples life in Christ. In fact, although it has not been discussed until now, you have been experiencing spiritual hunger right from the inception of your studies in discipleship. Without it, you would not have been motivated to study and seek to grow in poverty of spirit, spiritual mourning, and meekness.

Spiritual hunger is an intense desire you have for Christ's righteousness to affect your character and life (Ro. 3:21-23). It is this longing to know Christ that is at the foundation of all your upward growth in His likeness. Note in particular that the goal of spiritual hunger is transformation; a renewal of mind. If the purpose of a Christian is to glorify God by becoming like Christ, then spiritual hunger is the intense desire to accomplish that purpose. It is your willingness to allow the Holy Spirit freedom to work within you. It is your desire for Christ-likeness that invites the Spirit to make you into the image of Jesus (Ro. 8:29).

In the Book of Philippians, we discover the nature of spiritual hunger from the apostle Paul's experience. In chapter 3, the apostle says:

> What is more, I consider everything a loss compared to the surpassing greatness of knowing Christ Jesus my Lord, for whose sake I have lost all things. I consider them rubbish, that I may gain Christ and be found in him, not having a righteousness of my own that comes from the law, but that which is through faith in Christ—the righteousness that comes from God and is by faith. (Phil. 3:8-9)

In other words, Paul is saying that spiritual hunger is the motivating force that daily presses us "to know Christ, and the power of his resurrection and the fellowship of sharing in his sufferings, becoming like him in his death" (Phil. 3:10).

Sometimes, these feelings can be so intense that it seems as though we will never be fulfilled. However, God's promise to those who are spiritually hungry, to those who hunger and thirst after righteousness, is quite simple: "they shall be completely satisfied!" (Mt. 5:6, AB). Therefore, we can press on with the full assurance that our hunger is not in vain.

BIBLE STUDY GUIDE

Today's Bible Reading:
Philippians 3:4-14

1. In Philippians 3:4-6, Paul explains the high and proud position he had held before his conversion. In looking back at the important role in society that he played, what does Paul now say about his personal goals in life? Phil. 3:7-8 _____

_____

_____

_____

2. What did Paul desire more than anything else? Phil. 3:10 _____

_____

_____

_____

TODAY'S WORLD PRAYER EMPHASIS

AFRICA - ETHIOPIA
- Population: 52,569,000
- Religion: Traditional religions 6% - Non-religious/other 1% - Muslim 35%
  Protestant 14.1% - Catholic 0.75% - Marginal 0.03%
- Needs:
  In the early 1980s, Crossroads was able to generate more than $7 million in famine relief supplies. Crossroads also provided two helicopters which, over a 2-year period, supplied food to areas totally inaccessible by other means of transportation. Pray that the Ethiopians will remember the Christian witness of Crossroads' personnel who shared their faith at every opportunity.
  Pray that as this nation struggles politically and economically, the regional and national leaders will make wise decisions that will bring about peace instead of further conflict. Pray also that as struggles continue, Ethiopians will turn to Christ for hope.

WHAT PRODUCES SPIRITUAL HUNGER?

To fully understand what it means to hunger and thirst after righteousness, we must look at this principle within the context of the day in which Jesus lived.

Jesus was not speaking of a hunger and thirst that is satisfied by a mid-morning snack. He was speaking to people who lived on a subsistent wage. People who, if they were fortunate, ate meat once a week. Families who were never far from starvation and dehydration. To many in Christ's day (and many even today), the intensity of the words He chose to use regarding spiritual hunger and thirsting were readily understood.

Therefore, the question we must ask ourselves is: *Are we starving to know God?* This is the hunger Christ tells us can be filled.

The world tries to distract us from spiritual hunger pangs by filling us with desires for material things. This appetite for "things," and also for a "higher" or "better" position, subtly begins to take over our thoughts, crowding out our desire to know Christ as we should.

Sometimes, when this happens we have to be taken to a place where every prop has been removed and we can only cry out to God. It is here that God allows us to experience the desert as only the people of Jesus' day could understand. Here we are caught in a spiritual vacuum of desolation. A desert with intense, burning heat that parches our souls. In sandstorms, driven by winds that tear at the very fibers of our being—stinging our spiritual eyes and howling in our spiritual ears. We neither see nor hear God in our lives. Yet through this desert we learn to thirst for the righteousness of God and hunger for His presence.

As we wade through the sand day after day, we begin to notice that it becomes easier—the heat is not so intense, the winds are not so strong, the air is not so dry. Then, one day, we notice clouds forming from the east to the west, and God's Spirit begins to rain down on us. We drink as though we will never be filled. And as we look around us, we see that what was once a desolate place is now a lush garden, filled with the fruits of God's love and presence. We eat until we think we've had enough, but it seems as if the more we eat, the more hungry we become. For the more we know God, the more we desire to know Him better. This is the essence of hungering and thirsting after righteousness.

Our thirst for Christ's righteousness develops through daily growth in the Word, through trials, and through renewal. If we are to be truly transformed into the image of Jesus Christ, we must first be intensely hungry. Often, this hunger is brought about through desert experiences which come because of our own imperfection. However, God is not looking for us to be perfect. For through our imperfections He is able to teach us His ways and our desire to know Him increases. He is greatly pleased by our desire to know Him more fully.

■■■■■■■■■■■■■■■■■■■■■■■■■■■■■■■■■■■■■

BIBLE STUDY GUIDE

Today's Bible Reading: Mark 4:1-20

1. In the Parable of the Sower, Jesus describes four types of people who hear God's Word. What happens to the people who arc like seed sown among thorns and how do you think their situation destroys their hunger for God? Mk. 4:18-19 _____

_____

_____

2. Spiritual hunger develops through a daily growth in God's Word. How does Jesus describe this type of person? Mk. 4:20 _____

_____

_____

TODAY'S WORLD PRAYER EMPHASIS

LATIN AMERICA - EL SALVADOR
- Population: 5,943,000
- Religion: Non-religious/other2% - Protestant 20.6% - Roman Catholic 88.4%
  Marginal 1.8%
- Needs:
  Pray for this war-torn nation currently enjoying a fragile peace. Pray that the leadership will promote freedom for the gospel to be preached.
  Pray that the goal made by the Salvadoran Evangelical Confraternity of 3,400 new churches in El Salvador by the year 2000 may be reached and that El Salvador would truly be the Savior's. (*El Salvador* means "the Savior.")
  During the civil war, persecution of Christians was rampant. Pray that there is no bitterness left in the hearts of these people that might divide the body of Christ.

DISCIPLESHIP'S MOTIVATOR

THE
DESIRE TO
KNOW
PERSECUTION   CHRIST
PEACEMAKING   (Phil. 3:10)
PURITY
MERCY

MEEKNESS

SPIRITUAL MOURNING

POVERTY OF SPIRIT

THE PATHWAY OF DISCIPLESHIP

SPIRITUAL HUNGER

As we have discovered, spiritual hunger is the desire which motivates a disciple to follow the course that leads to effective Christian living and ministry.

It is the intense longing to know Christ that takes the disciple along the pathway of discipleship: poverty of spirit, spiritual mourning, meekness, mercifulness, purity, peacemaking, and possibly even persecution.

It is the motivation which says: Only as I realize my own poverty of spirit, am I rich in Christ. Only as I surrender to the discipline of God through spiritual mourning can I become strong in faith.

Only as I surrender my rights to the higher law of love (meekness) do I effectively serve God's purpose and claim the benefits of being His child. Only as I begin to see, feel, and meet human needs with love and mercy as God does can I really know His mercy personally. Only as I surrender to God's purification process can I really see and know Him. Only as I strive for love and oneness both with God and other people will my witness as a Christian be effective.

Once disciples are motivated by spiritual hunger, they begin to allow the process of discipline to take place. Spiritual hunger motivates us to press on toward the ultimate goal of our lives—to radiate the character of Christ to all people.

However, we must keep in mind that spiritual hunger becomes intense only as we cultivate it. The more we spend time with the Lord in personal as well as corporate worship, the more our desire to know Him increases. As the apostle Paul said, "Oh that I might know him..." (Phil. 3:10, paraphrase). In the original Greek, this statement meant to "experience" Christ, not just to know Him in the intellectual or historical sense. Spiritual hunger is the desire to experience Christ and His suffering, and ultimately His glory.

BIBLE STUDY GUIDE

Today's Bible Reading:
Matthew 5:6; Psalm 17, 119:10

1. What will happen to those who continue to develop a hunger for God?
Mt. 5:6 _____
_____
_____

2. What did David convey about those who seek and hunger for God? Psa.
17:15 _____
_____
_____
_____

3. With what intensity did David seek God through His Word? What does
it say to you about spiritual hunger? Psa. 119:10_____
_____
_____
_____
_____

TODAY'S WORLD PRAYER EMPHASIS

AFRICA - EQUATORIAL GUINEA
- Population: 497,000
- Religion: Tribal religion 5.1% - Non-religious/other 1% - Baha'i 0.4% - Muslim
    0.5% - Protestant 4.5% - Roman Catholic 87.8% - Marginal 0.7%
- Needs:
    This nation, devastated by war, will need years to recover. Virtually all educated
       people were either murdered or sent into exile. Pray that stability would be
       achieved and full religious freedom obtained.
    Pray for church leaders who have compromised their stands to avoid persecution and
       are now living in sin. Pray that the Holy Spirit will renew their hearts and that
       they will return to their First Love.
    Pray for the current ministry programs that are reaching out to the needy people
       despite restrictions placed upon them by the government. Pray that these pro-
       grams will reap a fruitful harvest.

CULTIVATING SPIRITUAL HUNGER

In this lesson, we will explore further what we call the Law of Spiritual Hunger—which says, "To have and maintain spiritual hunger, it must be cultivated."

Let's begin by looking at the basic differences between physical and spiritual hunger.

The first difference lies in the very nature of hunger.

Physical hunger is automatic. If we deprive ourselves of food, we automatically become hungry.

However, spiritual hunger must be cultivated. Depriving ourselves of spiritual food diminishes our desire for the things of God.

The second difference lies in how we gratify our hunger.

When we eat, our physical hunger is satisfied. The more we eat the more our physical hunger diminishes, until it finally disappears.

However, as we allow the flesh to be crucified through the discipline of sensory intake and feast upon the spiritual food of God's Word, our spiritual hunger actually intensifies. As we feast upon the Word, we are spiritually fed and satisfied. Yet, at the same time, we are given a deeper and stronger desire (spiritual hunger) to know Christ.

It is a paradox: the more we eat (know God), the more hungry we become (to know Him better).

If Christians are to maintain spiritual hunger, they must develop the following disciplines in their lives: (1) daily personal prayer; (2) daily personal study and meditation in the Word of God; and (3) a consistent effort to discipline their sensory intake (i.e., questionable movies, literature, television programs, music, and so forth) so as to starve the sinful nature. These disciplines will direct them to an even fuller personal knowledge of Christ.

In addition to these personal disciplines, if Christ's followers are going to maintain spiritual hunger, they must participate in meaningful fellowship and corporate worship with other believers on a regular basis. They must share and pray together with a group of Christians who deeply love and trust one another and who, therefore, are willing to bear one another's burdens.

Spiritual hunger also increases as His disciples discover and develop their spiritual gifts and become functioning members of the local body of believers. For in giving themselves to others in ministry and witness, their spiritual appetite is stimulated.

The more we are molded into the image Christ, the more we desire to know Him more fully. And He has promised that when we hunger after Him we will be filled.

■■■■■■■■■■■■■■■■■■■■■■■■■■■■■■

BIBLE STUDY GUIDE
Today's Bible Reading:
Isaiah 55:1-13

1. After the prophet Isaiah foretells the wonderful salvation brought by Jesus Christ (chapter 53), he then extends an invitation to all who hear. What is that invitation? Isa. 55:1 _____

_____

_____

_____

2. How does Isaiah describe so many people in the world today? Isa. 55:2

_____

_____

_____

_____

TODAY'S WORLD PRAYER EMPHASIS

EUROPE - FAEROE ISLANDS
- Population: 48,000
- Religion: Non-religious/other 6.6% - Protestant 93% - Roman Catholic 0.1%
    Marginal 0.3%
- Needs:
    Nominalism and liberal theology plague the national church. Pray for all who preach against this within the church. Currently, only about 8% of the Christians are church goers.
    Although Christianity is prevalent in this nation, the church has been subject to serious divisions. Consequently, there has been considerable damage done to the witness of the church. Pray for a fresh outpouring of the Holy Spirit that will heal the bitterness that is dividing the church.
    Pray with the Christians of these islands, that they will be able to send out 200 missionaries by the year 2000.

THE PSALMIST'S PORTRAYAL OF SPIRITUAL HUNGER

In our final two lessons on spiritual hunger, we are going to look at Psalm 42. This chapter more vividly portrays what it means to be hungry for God than any other portion of scripture.

The lesson to be learned from Psalm 42 is this: *Our hunger for the Lord is the only thing that will see us through times of great testing*. The path of discipleship is not easy, especially in times of God's molding and discipline. There is room for discouragement. Those, however, who desire to know Christ and the power of His resurrection and the fellowship of His sufferings, will persevere and trust God through it all.

The rest of today's lesson, and all of tomorrow's, will focus on a verse-by-verse commentary about what Psalm 42 says about spiritual hunger.

1. *Verses 1-2* "As the deer pants for the water, so I long for you, O God. I thirst for God, the living God. Where can I find him to come and stand before him?"

    Comment: These opening verses show us a man who is intensely hungry for the freshness of the living God in his life, yet he gives indication of a barrenness.

2. *Verse 3* "Day and night I weep for his help, and all the while my enemies taunt me. 'Where is this God of yours?' they scoff."

    Comment: Verse 3 gives us insight into the reason behind this man's feeling of barrenness. Hungry for God, he sought to know Him. But now, he finds himself in the state of mourning. Trials have encompassed him and those around him are saying, "Where is this God of yours?"

3. *Verses 4-6* "Take courage, my soul! Do you remember those times (but how could you ever forget them!) when you led a great procession to the Temple on festival days, singing with joy, praising the Lord? Why then be downcast? Why be discouraged and sad? Hope in God! I shall yet praise him for his help. Yet I am standing here depressed and gloomy, but I will meditate upon your kindness to this lovely land where the Jordan River flows and where Mount Hermon and Mount Mizar stand."

146

Comment: How glorious were those early days of our Christian experience. Every prayer was answered and God's presence was so keenly felt. Why in the process of growing up in Christ do we have to seemingly lose those early blessings? God's Word indicates that mourning is only for a season, so rather than dwell on our present problems, we should begin to praise Him. We know God is real and yet our emotions fail us. We should meditate upon the goodness of our God though we may not understand the purpose of our trial.

■■■■■■■■■■■■■■■■■■■■■■■■■■■■■■■■■■■■

BIBLE STUDY GUIDE
Today's Bible Reading: Psalm 42:1-11

1. In Matthew 5:6, Jesus described an intense type of hunger. How does the Psalmist describe the intensity of his own soul? Psa. 42:1-2 _____

_____

_____

2. How would you describe what the writer is personally experiencing in his life as he writes this Psalm? Psa. 42:3-4 _____

_____

3. Even though he is downcast, what spurs the Psalmist on? How would you relate this to the promise of Jesus in Matthew 5:6? Psa. 42:5-6 _____

_____

_____

TODAY'S WORLD PRAYER EMPHASIS

LATIN AMERICA - FALKLAND ISLANDS
- Population: 1,991
- Religion: Non-religious/other 13.1% - Protestant 76% - Roman Catholic 10.2% - Marginal 0.7%
- Needs:
  The traumatic invasion in 1982 brought many people face-to-face with Christ. Praise God for the 150 who made decisions to follow Him in 1991 at a crusade! Pray for lasting results in these lives.
  Pray for openness to the gospel on the large British military base here. Pray also that those who are Christians in the forces will be witnesses to their fellow soldiers.

WEEKEND DEVOTIONAL GUIDE

1. *Your prayer needs:*

• *Each week write down your newest prayer requests.*
• *After praying over them, transfer them to your main* God is Faithful
Prayer List *on page 162 and remember them daily.*
• *Each time a request is answered, draw a red line through it and date it
at the end.*

2. *Crossroads Christian Communications Prayer Need*

Pray for Crossroads' Financial Planning Department, that God would
give them wisdom to counsel Crossroads' friends and supporters spiritual and with financial wisdom as well.

3. *Lay Leadership International Prayer Need*

Pray for LLI's outreach to pastors and churches in the United States.
Pray that a great financial need of the ministry will be overcome so the
work can go on more effectively.

WEEKEND JOURNAL

Thoughts to reflect on and record:

1. Do I have the kind of spiritual hunger that desires to know Christ and experience His righteous character more than anything else?

2. Do the cares of life (i.e, my worries) and a desire for material things ever choke out my hunger for God?

3. Have I ever experienced the kind of spiritual hunger that others—like David and Paul—experienced? (i.e., Oh the bliss of the man who longs for total righteousness as a starving man longs for food, and a man perishing of thirst longs for water, for that man will be truly satisfied. [paraphrased from William Barclay's *The Gospel of Matthew: Daily Bible Study Series*, vol. 1, p 202.])

4. Knowing that spiritual hunger is not automatic, am I doing the things that will make me more hungry for God?

5. In times of discouragement, do I tend to give up seeking God or do I allow my trials to drive me to the Word where my spiritual hunger can be rekindled? Do I understand how an intense longing for God will see me through the worst of times?

THE CONCLUSION OF PSALM 42

Today we finalize our study of Psalm 42. As we found in yesterday's lesson, this is a Psalm that vividly depicts a person with an intense hunger and thirst for God. Let's now continue with our verse-by-verse study of the Psalm.

4. *Verses 7-8* "All your waves and billows have gone over me, and floods of sorrow pour upon me like a thundering cataract. Yet day by day the Lord also pours out his steadfast love upon me, and through the night I sing his songs and pray to God who gives me life."

Comment: These verses point out the conflict between the disciple's human emotions and what he knows to be the truth of God's Word. His trials are great. Only God can deliver him from his trouble. And in the midst of his depression he knows God loves him. He knows that he must sing songs, pray, and believe the promises of God.

5. *Verses 9-10* "'O God my Rock,' I cry, 'Why have you forsaken me? Why must I suffer these attacks from my enemies?' Their taunts pierce me like a fatal wound; again and again they scoff, 'Where is that God of yours?'"

Comment: Verse 9 shows the normal reaction that we experience during a period of mourning: "I believe, God, but why is this happening to me?" And then there are the "Job's comforters" who wrongly believe Christians should never face adversity and trial. They seek to point out our flaws, cloaking their judgmental remarks in superficial spirituality. The world also is looking at our situation and saying, "Where is that God of yours?"

6. *Verse 11* "But O my soul, don't be discouraged. Don't be upset. Expect God to act! For I know that I shall again have plenty of reason to praise him for all that he will do. He is my help! He is my God!"

Comment: We must not be discouraged by the trials of our faith; they are more precious than gold tried by fire. For the hungry, satisfaction will come. Expect God to act. Remember the words of Jesus, "What happiness there is for you who are now hungry, for you are going to be satisfied!" (Lk. 6:21, TLB).

We have discovered that spiritual hunger is the intense desire for righteousness in our daily living. It is the force in our lives which motivates us to know Christ more fully each day as we experience poverty of spirit, spiritual mourning, meekness, and so forth. Spiritual hunger is, indeed, the essential motivation of discipleship.

■■■■■■■■■■■■■■■■■■■■■■■■■■■■■■■■■■■■■

BIBLE STUDY GUIDE
Today's Bible Reading: Psalm 42:1-11

1. How does the Psalmist describe his trial? Who does he see as the One who has allowed it to happen? Ps. 42:7 _____

_____

_____

2. Through all of his trials, where is this writer's one true Anchor? Ps. 42:9

_____

_____

3. Even though he does not understand God's working in this situation, what is the Psalmist's attitude? Ps. 42:9-11 _____

_____

_____

_____

TODAY'S WORLD PRAYER EMPHASIS
EUROPE - FRANCE
- Population: 57,188,000
- Religion: Non-religious/other 19.2% - Muslim 7.7% - Jews 1.1% - Buddhist/Chinese religions 0.5% - Protestant 1.7% - Roman Catholic 68.1% - Other Catholic 0.1% - Orthodox 0.9% - Marginal 0.7%
- Needs:

France is in an incredible state of spiritual bondage. Though there are many who call themselves "Christians," for most it is only a nominal religion. Intellectualism, rationalism, involvement in the occult, and individualism, are only a few of the barriers that separate these people from a personal relationship with Jesus Christ. Pray fervently that the Holy Spirit will melt the hearts of the French people that they may receive true wisdom and love that is evident in a life lived for Jesus Christ.

The unreached of France are too numerous to list. Pray that all who have not heard or have hardened their hearts to the gospel might be saved.

Pray for ministries to college students in this country. The intellectual elite scoff at the simplicity of Christianity, but many students are beginning to sense a need that cannot be filled by material wealth. Pray that the outreaches on these campuses may rejoice in a fruitful harvest.

Lesson 62

LOOKING BACK ON MEEKNESS AND LIFE'S HIGHEST AUTHORITY

In the first section of this book, we learned that meekness involves an upward or vertical attitude towards God.

This attitude involves submission to God's Word, submission to human authority, and submission to God's leading by the Holy Spirit.

Included in meekness is also a believer's horizontal or outward relationships with others.

With the help of the Holy Spirit we must cultivate an all-encompassing attitude of humility and gentleness toward all people. This type of meekness is not easy because quite often it runs contrary to the values of society.

Yet as we surrender to the Holy Spirit, meekness can be produced in our lives. Our rebellious self-will can be reshaped and channeled into an attitude of obedience to God.

In seeking meekness, we have the example of Jesus Christ to help us. He was meek and lowly.

Moses and Paul also stand out as people who, through God's discipline, exemplified meekness in their lives. In fact, Moses was the only person in the Bible, other than Jesus, to be called "meek".

In dealing with the areas of our lives that are involved in our upward submission to God, we must look our highest authority—God's Holy Word.

Because the Bible is the only infallible guide in a Christian's faith (what they believe) and practice (what they do), it is extremely important that we learn how to interpret Scripture correctly.

Although the Holy Spirit is our only true Teacher, certain guides and tools can and should be used to help us understand God's Word correctly. Such things as church history, denominational history, the body of Christ today, and the ministry of the pastor-teacher—as well as interpretive tools like principles of hermeneutics—greatly help us in our understanding of what God is saying through His Word.

May the Holy Spirit help each one of us grow in meekness toward God in every area of life.

Only then can we truly become all that Christ desires us to be in both our faith and our witness.

BIBLE STUDY GUIDE

Today's Bible Reading:
Read and reaffirm the following truths;
then write down your thoughts.

1. There are areas of the sinful nature that remain in me and are rebellious. Also, there are things in every believer's life that need God's training and discipline. Therefore, I must be open to the Lord's dealing with me so that I can grow more and more in His meekness.Ro. 7:21-23_____

_____

_____

_____

2. The Word of God is the highest authority in my life. 2 Tim. 3:16-17____

_____

_____

_____

3. In order to correctly interpret the Word of God, I must study the Scriptures, depend on the Holy Spirit to show me God's truths, and check out my interpretations with the authorities and helps God has given me. 2 Tim. 2:15 _____

_____

_____

_____

TODAY'S WORLD PRAYER EMPHASIS

CARIBBEAN - FRENCH GUIANA
- Population: 130,000
- Religion: Nonreligious/other 8.8% - Spiritist 2% - Muslim 1.5% - Baha'i 0.8% - Protestant 5.8% - Roman Catholic 80% - Marginal 1.1%
- Needs.

  Pray that a translation of the New Testament will quickly be completed. Only a handful of Guianese Creole speakers are active Christians, and currently there is no New Testament translation in their language.

  The most responsive peoples to the gospel message have been the Haitians, Antilleans, Hmong, and Brazilians. Pray that God will call more men and women to minister in this nation to reach these people and others.

  Pray for the least reached peoples—the Amerindians, the Chinese, and the French and European communities.

Lesson 63
LOOKING BACK ON SUBMISSION TO HUMAN AUTHORITY AND THE HOLY SPIRIT

In section two we discovered that meekness involves our submission and obedience to human authorities. God has instituted civil, family, and church authorities in the world. True believers must recognize the God-given right of these authorities to rule and that they should submit to them as part of God's will for their lives.

There are occasions, however, when human authority seeks to rise above the authority of God's Word. In such cases, Christians have no choice but to obey God's Word rather than the human authority. This may bring persecution. Yet meekness also necessitates non-retaliation and love.

Sometimes there also arises conflicts between human authorities and what one feels is the leading of God's Spirit. Rather than disobeying the authority in question, meekness entails praying for a change in the authority's attitude; an alternate plan of action; or, at times, even the removal of the offending authority.

In the church we usually find three levels of authority that are common. There is the level that assumes overall leadership, known in the Early Church as "elders." Under this is a second level that involves itself in administrating various areas of practical service—known in the Early Church as "deacons". Finally, there is the gifted membership which includes everyone. True believers should seriously follow the leadership of the church in matters of what they believe and how they conduct themselves in their witness before world.

Finally, we looked at the importance of being led by God's Holy Spirit. This area, however, can lead to serious problems unless we keep certain principles in full view.

Through a daily life of prayer, we will begin to recognize the voice of God's Spirit within us. This needs to be tested, however, by the Word of God. Any true leading of the Holy Spirit will never conflict with the principles of God's Word. It is also good to ask God to confirm His leading by speaking to you about the same thing through His Word.

As we seek to understand God's leading, it is good to test what we are hearing by consulting other godly confidants who treat what we tell them with confidentiality. One should keep in mind, however, that there are certain levels in our relationships where only confidential things can be shared. Jesus maintained at least 5 levels of relationships—the multitudes, the 70, the 12, the 3 (Peter, James, and John), and the 1 (John).

Also, if we feel God is leading us into areas that involve others, we must test that leading by how cooperative the others are. We must be patient. Sometimes leaders who have a vision or leading from God and must wait, as Joshua did, for the stubborn people to come around.

Finally, testing circumstances for the right timing is very important. If doors arc not opening, it may be an indication that it is not yet God's time to move. However, we should be careful not to be ruled by circumstances. Ultimately, there does come a time when the leading of the Holy Spirit has been confirmed. It is then time to step out in faith and accomplish the impossible.

■■■■■■■■■■■■■■■■■■■■■■■■■■■■■■■■■■■■■■

BIBLE STUDY GUIDE
Today's Bible Reading:
Read and reaffirm the following truths.

1. A Christian must always be subject to the governing authorities within society. Ro. 13

2. A believer must be subject to God's model of love and submission in the family. Eph. 5:51-6:4

3. A Christian must be subject to God's authority in the Church, recognizing the leader's responsibility to equip them in God's Word and wholeness and helping them grow in purity of life. Heb. 13:17

4. A Christian must be led of the Holy Spirit by weighing the inner voice against God's Word, counsel from godly confidants, and unity and cooperation when other believers are involved. Ro. 8:14

5. A Christian should not usurp human authority based upon a personal leading. Rather, one should seek a creative alternative, wait patiently for the authority to change, or pray that God will remove the barriers all together. Dan. 1:8-16

6. When human authority oversteps its boundaries and tries to usurp the authority of God's Word, that authority must be disobeyed, regardless of the consequences. Acts 4:19

TODAY'S WORLD PRAYER EMPHASIS

PACIFIC - FRENCH POLYNESIA
- Population: 200,000
- Religion: Chinese religions 0.6% - Non-religious/other 14.8% - Protestant 41% - Roman Catholic 33% - Marginal 10.4%
- Needs:
  Pray for a spiritual revolution to take place among those Catholics and Protestants who are only nominal Christians. Finding a Christian with a vital and personal faith is rare. There are only a handful of evangelical churches.
  Pray for the unreached peoples. The gospel is hardly known on many of these islands.

Lesson 64
LOOKING BACK ON HUMILITY & GENTLENESS

In section two, we saw that in addition to being submitted to God's authority, meekness also involves how we relate to others.

The new nature of Christ within us desires to bring forth an attitude of humility and gentleness.

Humility involves serving the needs of others without possessing any ulterior motive. Whomever we minister to—be it a saint, a sinner, or even our enemy—we do so because Christ's love dwells within us.

Christian leaders in society, as well as leaders in the church, also have a divine responsibility to serve the needs of those under them. In doing so, they are reversing the worldly attitude of obtaining personal gain by serving only the needs of the person at the top.

In addition to being humble, Jesus, our Great Example, is also gentle with His creation.

In Matthew 9, He saw people being harassed by Satan and had compassion for them, rather than judgement.

He sought for laborers who would react to every situation with gentleness and love.

The flesh can be harsh, uncaring, forceful, coercive, and manipulative. Christians, however, are called to gentleness and non-retaliation.

As strange as this may seem to the world's ideas for gaining control, acts of gentleness bring God's love and words to the hearts of men and women. Only the way of meekness, through humility and gentleness, will win the world for Christ.

Christ humbled Himself. He came from the highest position in the universe to one of the lowest positions on earth to serve all people in every strata of society.

Jesus, the Son of God, faced the most socially disgraceful type of death—crucifixion—solely for the purpose of serving the needs of a lost and hurting world. Yet throughout the injustice of dying for a crime never committed, Jesus' only "retaliation" was to pray, "Father, forgive them for they know not what they do."

As believers, Jesus asks that we take upon us His yoke of meekness. His call is for us to learn His ways of relating to others, for He is "gentle and humble of heart" (Mt. 11:29).

BIBLE STUDY GUIDE

Today's Bible Reading:
Read and affirm the following truths;
then write down your thoughts.

1. A Christian needs to grow in humility, which involves serving others regardless of their position in life as Christ did. Phil. 2:3-4 _____
_____
_____

2. Christian leaders and helpers must see the world as Christ did—people harassed by the devil without a shepherd to protect them. Then they must go forth as co-laborers with Christ to heal and restore people to Him. Mt. 9:35-38 _____
_____
_____

3. Christians must learn to forgive and be non-retaliatory and non-vindictive. They must learn to be gentle and loving to all people, even their enemies. Lk. 6:27-38_____
_____
_____

4. Christians must follow the example of Christ who called them saying, "I am meek and gentle of heart." Mt. 11:29 _____
_____
_____

TODAY'S WORLD PRAYER EMPHASIS

EUROPE - GIBRALTAR
- Population: 31,000
- Religion: Muslim 10% - Jewish 1.7% - Hindu 1.1% - Protestant 7.9% - Roman Catholic 66.7% - Marginal 0.9%
- Needs:
  Pray for the Protestant witness. Pray the Holy Spirit will make the truth of the gospel come alive in the hearts of the church, and that the Christians may boldly witness to this nation.
  Pray for an outreach to Moroccan Muslims who number some 7,000. Pray that these people may be brought to the Lord.
  Praise God for the small group of Arab believers who meet regularly! Pray that they may reach out to their fellow immigrants.

Lesson 65
LOOKING BACK ON SPIRITUAL HUNGER...

In the final lessons of Book 3, we dealt with the fourth Beatitude: *Blessed are those who hunger and thirst for righteousness, for they will be filled.*

Spiritual hunger is our great motivator. It spurs us on to further growth in the character of Christ. Spiritual hunger is an intense desire to know Christ that takes us along the pathway of discipleship—through poverty of spirit, spiritual mourning, meekness, mercifulness, purity, peacemaking, and possibly even persecution.

Spiritual hunger, however, is not like physical hunger. Whereas in the physical realm our feelings of hunger are automatic, in the spiritual realm, hunger for the things of God must be cultivated. Cultivation of spiritual hunger is possible only as individuals give themselves to feeding on spiritual things. The more they take in, the more hungry they become.

In Psalm 42, we saw one man's spiritual hunger as he went through a desert experience. Often in the midst of our greatest trials, we hunger for and eventually feel God's presence as never before.

It is our prayer at Crossroads and LLI that your hunger for God will be "satisfied" as you continue on the path of discipleship that Christ taught us in the Beatitudes. May your hunger for God spur you on to be all that you desire to be as a Christian, and more.

...AND AHEAD TO MERCIFULNESS

In Book 4 of our *Life by Design* series, we will be looking into the fifth Beatitude: *Blessed are the merciful.*

In this study, we will come to an understanding of how God has given each one of us gifts so that we might become agents of some particular area of His grace and mercy.

Together we will learn more about ourselves as we participate in a self-analysis of our own spiritual giftedness. This type of study will help us better understand God's will for our lives in light of the gifts He has given us.

BIBLE STUDY GUIDE

Today's Bible Reading:
Please re-read and affirm the following truth;
then write down your thoughts.

1. A Christian who is growing is one who is cultivating an intense hunger for God—a hunger and thirst that Christ described as one that a person would feel who is without food and water in the desert. Mt. 5:6 _____

_____

_____

2. In Psalm 42, the Psalmist shows the type of hunger for God that sustains us through trials and brings us to the fulfillment of Christ's promise of satisfaction. Ps. 42:1-11_____

_____

_____

3. Paul expresses the type of spiritual hunger that every disciple should believe for. Phil. 3:7-10 _____

_____

_____

TODAY'S WORLD PRAYER EMPHASIS
NORTH AMERICA - GREENLAND
- Population: 58,000
- Religion: Non-religious/other 1.4% - Baha'i 0.4% - Protestant 97.6% - Roman Catholic 0.2% - Marginal 0.4%
- Needs:

   Though the majority of the poulation claims to be Christian, most have no concept of a personal relationship with Jesus Christ. Pray for renewal and new life for every person in this small nation.

   Modernity has adversely affected Greenland. Pray that the translated Bible will be read, and the people will see new birth rather than the devastation of suicide and alcoholism they currently face each day.

WEEKEND DEVOTIONAL GUIDE

1. *Your prayer needs:*

• *Each week write down your newest prayer requests.*
• *After praying over them, transfer them to your main* God is Faithful
Prayer List *on page 162 and remember them daily.*
• *Each time a request is answered, draw a red line through it and date it
at the end.*

2. *Crossroads Christian Communications Prayer Need*

Pray for the personal ministry to visitors and team members at Crossroads. Pray that all who minister will experience renewed strength as
they daily pour out their lives for others.

3. *Lay Leadership International Prayer Need*

Pray that this cooperative venture between Crossroads and LLI will
bless people around the world and give other ministries a tool that will
help them in their work of evangelism and discipleship.

WEEKEND JOURNAL

Thoughts to reflect on and record:

1. At times when I don't understand the reason for the struggle I am facing, do I affirm my faith in God to see me through as the Psalmist did in Psalm 42:1-11?

2. I need to once more evaluate my openness to the Lord's molding and discipline, as well as my belief in and obedience to God's Word as the greatest authority in my life. Do I spend enough time studying the Word? Do I listen to God's guiding authorities and helps to keep myself from error?

3. Am I subject to God's ordained human authorities in my life? Do I wait on God in order to be led by His Holy Spirit?

4. Am I growing in my understanding and daily practice of what it means to serve others, regardless of who they are? Am I growing in and reacting with gentleness, even to those who are spiteful with me?

5. Am I developing the hunger for God that will ultimately fill me with the knowledge and satisfaction that knowing Christ more fully brings?

GOD IS FAITHFUL PRAYER LIST
Remove Your Mountains Through Prayer

To be used with your daily Weekend Devotional Guide and Journal

REQUEST	REMARKS	DATE ASKED	DATE ANSWERED
DAVID - PAUL SHAUNA. MID. JULY 98	HEALTH- REIHEALTH·BABY	14TH -	

Suggestions:
1. Ask specifically. Put God in a "yes" or "no" situation.
2. Pray over each request each day.
3. Keep praying until the answer comes.
4. When your request is answered, draw a red line through it.
5. Make extra copies of this form for additional requests.